GROWING A FAMILY

Where People Really Like Each Other

GROWING A FAMILY

Where People Really Like Each Other

Karen Dockrey

BETHANY HOUSE PUBLISHERS
MINNEAPOLIS, MINNESOTA 55438

Published by Bethany House Publishers
A Ministry of Bethany Fellowship, Inc.
11300 Hampshire Avenue South
Minneapolis, Minnesota 55438

Printed in the United States of America.

Library of Congress Cataloging-in-Publication Data

Dockrey, Karen, 1955–
    Growing a family where people really like each other / Karen Dockrey.
      p. cm.
    ISBN 1-55661-671-6
      1. Parent and child. 2. Parent and child—Religious aspects—Christianity.
3. Family. 4. Family—Religious life. 5. Cheerfulness. I. Title.
HQ755.85.D63   1996
248.8'45—dc20   95–45077
                                                      CIP

To my daughters,
who teach the meaning of delight

KAREN DOCKREY's strongest qualification to write this book is her daily walk with you in the adventure of parenting. She has written twenty-five other books for families and teenagers including the *Holman Student Bible Dictionary*, *When a Hug Won't Fix the Hurt: Walking With Your Child Through Crisis*, and together with her daughter *You'll Never Believe What They Told Me: Trusting God Through Serious Illness*. She has a Master of Divinity from Southern Baptist Theological Seminary. She works with teenagers and parents across the nation. She has served two churches as minister to youth. She currently teaches Bible studies and trains leaders twice a week at her church. But her strongest desire is to please God in her parenting. She speaks from the trenches, as a fellow parent who is still a student of family happiness. She and her husband, Bill, parent two children who have faced such happiness stealers as pediatric cancer and profound hearing loss. More importantly they share daily joys such as interest in each other, hysterical mistakes, celebrated successes, and delightful friends.

CONTENTS

*And my God will meet all your needs according to his glorious
riches in Christ Jesus.*

—Philippians 4:19

Introduction

WELCOME TO THE ADVENTURE

Love must be sincere. Hate what is evil; cling to what is good.

—Romans 12:9

Perhaps you've been dreaming about parenting since you were a child yourself. Or maybe you started to dream the day you learned you were expecting a baby. Somehow—sometime between the day you started dreaming and the time your dream came true—you grew a little confused. In real life parenting can seem more like a nightmare than a dream. It starts with a crying baby who keeps you up at night. Then come the terrible twos followed by run-to-the-ball-field-every-afternoon elementary years. You agonize through the hormones of early adolescence and worry when your teens get their driver's licenses. Finally one day you drive them to college or to their own apartment and come home to an empty house. *Where did the time go?* you lament. A lump forms in your throat and tears well in your eyes. *I miss them!*

The good news is you don't have to settle for a nightmare. You can choose the happy dream. You can focus on the gurgles of babies, the inventiveness of two-year-olds, the wisdom of children, and the spiritual insight of teenagers. You can enjoy each stage, each year, each day with each of your one-of-a-kind children. Rather than miss your kids, you can learn from them and delight in them. You can build the kind of closeness and mutuality that lasts a lifetime. And you can wrap your family in a blanket of love that lasts for generations.

Take the dream a little further. What if every child was not only cherished by his parents and by God, but also believed and relied on that cherishing? And what if, as an outgrowth of that love, each child treated others with kindness, respect, and true enjoyment? What if each child believed that wherever he went he held a crucial role in growing God's happiness? And then what if these children had parents who showed them how to bring happiness through the words they speak, the actions they choose, the way they solve problems, the way they manage sadness? These children would recognize that their words and actions make a difference. They would choose to work hand in hand with God to make that difference a positive one. They would live their lives to answer Jesus' prayer "Our Father . . . your kindom come, your will be done on earth as it is in heaven" (Matthew 6:9–10).

Choosing the dream won't be easy. Everywhere you look you'll see fellow parents whining about their kids and you'll feel tempted to join in and top their horror stories. But what good will that do? Complaining about your kids is like letting Scrooge plan Christmas. It steals fun. It makes you feel oppressed and makes your kids feel like dirt. So refuse to whine, to get down on your kids, or to feed misery.

Instead, stubbornly approach each day as a never-to-be-repeated adventure with your kids. Go in with your eyes wide open—there will be trees to ski around, bumps to navigate, and icy snow in your face. But there will also be the brisk thrill of mastering a run you've struggled with before, the warmth of the sun on your face, and the soothing flow of honest conversation after a time of coldness. Start today to reject the view that says children are nuisances sent to distract your life and tear up your possessions. Instead, enjoy your children as imperfect but delightful people who can enrich your life in countless ways while you do the same for them.

Come live the adventure!

1

I'D RATHER DO IT ANOTHER DAY

*Offer your bodies as living sacrifices, holy and pleasing to God—
this is your spiritual act of worship.*

—Romans 12:1

All I wanted was a shower and my bed.

My daughters and I had spent four days sightseeing in Washington, D.C. Eager to get home to Dad, we planned to drive three hours to knock a little time off the next day's trip. Thirty minutes out of town we realized we'd forgotten our garment bag. We drove back for it. One hour added to our drive. We hit construction at the northern edge of Virginia. Another hour-long delay. When my daughters said they were hungry—it was nearly 7:30—I promised that if they could just stay patient until we got to the hotel, we'd swim, and eat at a fun restaurant. We munched on snacks and looked forward to a refreshing dip in the pool.

An hour later we pulled up at our chosen hotel. The parking lot was curiously full. There was one room left, a smoking room with a broken toilet lid. Wearily I asked if we could check the room before taking it. It didn't smell too badly and the crack had been glued. We took the room.

"Whew! Glad we came to our hotel first—we got the very last room," I said with more enthusiasm than I felt. "Let's get something to eat!" Inwardly I thanked God for taking care of us, but chided myself for not making a reservation.

"Where's the nearest McDonald's?" my daughter asked the hotel clerk.

"Turn left at our driveway and then take the first left."

Sounded easy enough. We took two lefts, but saw no golden arches. After driving a couple miles down a dark and twisting road, I decided I must have taken a wrong turn. There were no lights anywhere ahead to indicate civilization, and I wasn't excited about getting lost at night without my husband.

We returned to the main road and searched both directions. No McDonald's, no fast-food places of any kind. We recognized one sit-down restaurant and arranged to carry out hamburgers. That, I reasoned, would take much less time than eating in. We had a swim to take. Ten minutes led to fifteen, and then to twenty. We explored the lobby until we had it memorized.

My daughters spotted a display full of jawbreaker suckers that rotated on a battery-operated motor. "Can we get these for dessert?" they asked without a bit of whining. "It'll be great. We won't have to lick—just enjoy!"

I looked at the price tag. Three dollars apiece! *Six dollars for two suckers?* The frugal me said no. *But this could make the wait easier,* another part of me said. *The girls have been so patient. Besides, this may be like the five-dollar hot dog on the Washington, D.C. mall—something they'll talk about forever because it's a rare splurge.*

The girls gleefully agreed to split with me the cost of the amazing twirling jawbreakers. "Why don't we eat backwards tonight," I suggested. "Start with the jawbreakers first."

"Really?" they asked with a look that said, "Is this the same mother who makes us clean our plates before dessert?"

"Really," I responded. I grinned at their looks of absolute ecstasy. The humming jawbreaker motors sounded like angels singing as we waited another fifteen minutes. As they started on their jawbreakers a clerk offered us a checker game to play until our food came.

Amid a jovial game of checkers our food arrived. On the way to the van we discovered our french fries were missing. Five more minutes and we had french fries, but no drinks. Finally everything was together and we trekked back to the van, jawbreaker motors humming merrily.

I dreaded telling the girls it was now too late to swim. I knew the pool closed at 10:00. It was 9:57. And it had begun to rain.

"That's okay! We'll swim another time," my eldest daughter, Emily, said. "This jawbreaker is great. I'm trying the top-lick method and Sarah the side-lick method to see which way it lasts longest. And I think I've figured out a way to reuse it. You just put another sucker in this hole. Or we could use a nail to put a hole in a regular jawbreaker and use this stick. But that might crack the jawbreaker. Well, we'll experiment until we find a way that works. Thanks, Mom. These are great."

What started out to be a disastrous meal in a smoky-smelling hotel room on a rainy night turned out to be a marvelous adventure. The girls ate their semi-warm, soggy food as if it were hot off the grill.

I got to bed three hours later than I wanted to. But my bed was cozier and my dreams happier than they would have been without the jawbreaker surprise. The girls carefully tucked those treasured jawbreakers into their wrappers to savor them again the next morning. Then I slipped into sleep, savoring the sweet constancy of God's provision.

Choose Adventure, Not Disaster

What made this night so wonderful? Was it candy? Not really. It was novelty, kindness, and an attitude of adventure.

Was I a superparent? Far from it. I had to sit hard on my impatience to keep it from exploding. I had to fight to show kindness to the restaurant employees when I felt like saying, "What are you doing back in that kitchen? Can't you see I have hungry children? Did you have to go out and kill the cow? How long can it take to cook three small hamburgers?" But along with those urges to vent I heard soft promptings to show love. I scarcely recognized that God was speaking. In His power I spoke gentle words to my children when I felt like sleeping. Through His mercy I spoke encouraging words to the restaurant employees when I felt like snapping.

I came dangerously close to disobeying. But close on the heels of those tiny obediences, I experienced the delight of God's gifts: laughter when we could have had tears, patient sisters who overcame their tendency to argue when hungry, compassionate people in the restaurant lobby who offered a game of checkers while we waited. Small kindnesses unleashed floods of goodness. I stood back in awe at our God, then trembled at how frequently I fail to obey.

What made that night good wasn't an inborn goodness—mine

or my girls'. It was choice. With God's power I chose to treat my children the way God treats me, speaking to them with the same kindness my tired soul needed. I chose to treat our mishaps as adventures rather than as excuses for misery.

Simple, caring actions carry eternal significance. The memory of that night and others like it empower my children to manage inconvenience with gentleness and humor rather than blaming and biting. It equips them to watch for joy in every encounter. No magic—just truth. Kindness bred kindness. Care deepened joy. What worked was finding fun in the middle of catastrophe. It was realizing we'd never get this particular night back to do over again—so we might as well make the best of it.

How much nicer that evening might have been if we'd had a meal on time, a room without lingering smoke, and a quiet swim in a cloud-free night. I could have put my feet up and enjoyed watching my children frolic in the water.

But that wasn't the day we had.

We faced forgotten luggage, snail-paced traffic, steady rain, stale smoke, and gnawing hunger. But we weren't alone: "Thanks be to God, who always leads us in triumphal procession in Christ and through us spreads everywhere the fragrance of the knowledge of him" (2 Corinthians 2:14). The fragrance of God pervaded our evening with a perfection I couldn't have begun to imagine. He gave us gifts far beyond my canned definition of a "nice" evening.

Perfect days come along once every million years or so. We can take the days we have and enjoy them. Or we can waste away our days with whining and feuding. We don't have the option of trading these days for better ones. We do have the option of calling on God and then delighting in the surprises He brings.

Work Toward God's Kingdom

Each day families face two possibilities: They move closer together, or they drift apart. They practice forgiveness, or let irritations dig in and fester. They learn to like each other even more, or find even more things to dislike.

Growing a family where people enjoy each other is living the answer to Jesus' prayer, "Our Father . . . your kingdom come, your will be done on earth as it is in heaven" (Matthew 6:9–10). We work with our children toward making life on this earth as good as it will be in heaven. Hand-in-hand with God we promote choices, words, and actions that honor Him. We model for our children strategies for living lives given to God in the good times and the bad. With day-by-day loving actions, we build a foundation of joy and security on which to grow happiness, other-centeredness, and goodness. Faith is another word for this foundation. This faith is unshaken when the world delivers hurt. This faith refuses to be puffed up when things go well—instead it thanks God, the giver of all good gifts (James 1:17).

Enjoying life with our children isn't seeing life as a party or ignoring the bad. It's approaching life as a team, deepening joys because we do life together, making magnificent the mundane. Together we find and live God's joy. Together we help each other through the hard times. Together we give privacy to the one who needs it. As a family team we recognize what's worth getting upset about, and we save our sadness and anger for those issues. We attack problems with positiveness and discipline with consistency rather than bite into each other. We meet each other's need with care rather than condescension.

> I stood back in awe at our God, who has created a wondrous world where small kindnesses unleash floods of goodness.

A family that enjoys each other is an empowered family. They experience goodness. They know life as God meant it to be. They are able to say along with Paul, "I have learned the secret of being content in any and every situation" (Philippians 4:12).

Enjoying Our Kids

Contentment doesn't come naturally to me. I'm much better at whining and complaining. But through good friends and steady love, God is teaching me a better way.

I once remarked to a friend that I could hardly wait until I had a second child. Her incredulous look startled me. "I don't understand," she said. "All you do is complain about the one you have."

It's All In How You Say It

We parents set the tone of an event by the words and attitudes we show. How do the expressions on the left promote adventure rather than whining? What other words would you choose?

Adventure Words	Whining Words
"There's not much leftover smoke."	"This hotel room stinks!"
"Wow! We've never had supper this late!"	"It's about time we ate!"
"We can have an indoor picnic!"	"The rain spoiled our day."
"You're tired, so work hard to talk calmly."	"Quit that arguing!"
"We'll tell a great story about this storm!"	"I'm miserably wet!"
"This is a quiet kind of fun."	"This is boring."

I recoiled, stunned and hurt. But almost as instantl
the truth in her words. I was much quicker to say, "
me up all night" than, "Oh how I love my baby's sw
complaining words didn't match my heart feelings. Even in my
frustrated moments, I'd count nothing more precious than sharing
life with my daughter, discovering together how to live for God.

I had learned too well, however, a pattern of kid-criticism.
Rather than say what I liked about my child, I complained about her
latest illness or the way she pulled every book off the bookshelf before choosing the one she wanted to read. I didn't like illnesses. They
hurt my daughter and robbed sleep from both of us. But to be honest, I considered it a privilege to rock my weeping infant until she
comfortably slept on my shoulder. And though the mountain of
books was a bother to pick up, I delighted in my daughter's adora-
tion for words and pictures. She'd study those books with such rapt
attention that I could seldom resist joining her on the floor for a
good read. My words never told this story, never showed this part
of my heart. The "words of my mouth" had not been "pleasing" to
God. (Psalm 19:14)

Equally important, my words had discredited my child and discouraged those who listened to me. I had let whining dominate my
conversation and seep into the way I viewed my child.

I thanked my friend for her honesty. I sheepishly confessed she
was right. I had been pretty negative. "I enjoy my daughter much
more than I say," I acknowledged to her and to myself.

Her response reassured me and motivated me. "No problem,"
she said with grace. "We all complain sometimes."

As I mulled what my friend had said—the sting didn't go away
for a while—I made a commitment to God to recognize, talk about,
and *enjoy* the good in my family. I asked Him to empower me. *Growing a family where people like each other had to start with me.* We parents are the catalysts.

As God made me sensitive to my own words and attitudes toward
my children, I've discovered that "word-bashing," that continual
barrage of condemning and critical words, isn't reserved for child
abusers or non-Christians. It's something multitudes of caring parents do unless they make a conscious commitment to do otherwise.
We hear kid-criticism almost as often in church hallways as we do
in grocery stores and at ball fields:

*How could you do something so stupid! Pick that up before
anyone sees it!*
Don't ask him to lead that lesson—he'll just mess it up.
Just wait until he's two.
What's she going to be like when she's a teenager?
There won't be any children there, will there?

I'm not sure why we say those things. Maybe we're embarrassed by our children's mistakes. Maybe we fear how it reflects on our parenting and our spiritual maturity. Perhaps we see so few people who enjoy their families that we think we're strange if we do. Possibly we don't know how to compliment. Or maybe we don't realize that the way we treat our children is a holy calling.

Something inside us must know it's wrong to slight and discredit our kids because we follow many of our words with "Just teasing" or, "You know I don't mean to be rough on you." Another part of us, however, still fears giving our kids bloated heads if we say nice things about them. *If we like them too much*, we wonder, *won't they become spoiled and selfish?*

Not at all.

Spoiled is letting our children be cruel. It's allowing them to have their own way rather than consider the needs of those around them. It's laughing at everything they do whether cruel or caring.

Enjoyment is giving our children the privilege of choosing right, even if it's not the way they initially would choose. It's equipping children with structure, encouragement, and Bible knowledge, so they can experience the pure pleasure of good choices, actions, and attitudes.

Spoiled is providing surplus possessions. It's giving our children whatever they ask for. Spoiled is letting our children believe that things and money give power and security.

Enjoyment is giving ourselves and our time to our children more often than we give money or things. Enjoyment is showing the power of life lived out in Jesus Christ. It's providing a faith foundation, a security that comes with daily acts of obedience to God.

Spoiled is allowing our children to get whatever they want however they can get it. It's letting them miss the joy of watching another's face light up when they do something kind. It's letting them bypass the togetherness that grows when they selflessly see another's need and meet it.

Spoiled and selfish happen when we make our children the center of attention.

Enjoyment is prompting our children to seek good for everyone. It's helping them see the needs surrounding them, needs as simple as a schoolmate who needs an invitation to play. It's showing our children how to delight in obeying God. It's cultivating caring words and Christlike attitudes.

Enjoyment happens as our children look outside themselves to involve everyone rather than pick on a few with cruelty. It happens as they choose to be selfless instead of piggish, considerate rather than impulsive.

Enjoyment means

- building wonder instead of whining;
- seeing adventure rather than catastrophe;
- growing delight rather than giving in to dread;
- expressing disagreement calmly rather than bickering;
- focusing on people rather than predicaments;
- making the mood by the little things we say and do;
- cherishing each day as a gift from God.

Notice What You're Doing

My friends Earl and Elizabeth raised three honor students who give joy to people of all ages. These three young adults are uniquely selfless, specifically kind, and definitely caring. Just being around them reminds you of God's goodness. I asked Earl the secret to parenting his fine children. "I brag on them," he said, "and let them hear what I say."

Far from giving kids big heads, enjoying our children equips them to believe God's love and heed God's commands. True treasuring gives children the security they need to give up conceit to become self-giving. It provides the tools to reject evil and embrace good. It grows solid relationships rather than surface ones. As our children feel genuinely cared for, they discover ways to approach all aspects of life positively. They find the power they need to serve their Savior. This isn't making children the center of the universe but pointing them toward the Center of the Universe, our God who cherishes and empowers them.

Enjoyment is recognizing that negative words undermine a child's joy and security as certainly as waves pull sand from the seashore. The shoreline may look invincible, but each time we discredit a child we steadily erode that child's foundation. We convince him that neither we nor God care one bit about him. So why should he even try doing good or growing faith?

Enjoyment chooses to deliberately build a foundation of security and joy in each of our children, a foundation that believes, "I matter to God and to my family." It's recognizing each event as a never-to-be-repeated opportunity for growth in Jesus. We teach our children how to please Christ by doing so ourselves and by coupling explanations with actions: "We've got to drive an extra hour because we forgot the garment bag. We all wish it were different, but we might as well make the best of it. Complaining will just make us more miserable, so let's pop in some music and sing."

> Enjoying our children isn't making children the center of the universe but pointing them toward the Center of the Universe, our God who cherishes and equips them for the good and bad of life.

Enjoyment is what we do to *make* our days good. It isn't something for times when we have extra energy or when the days are good. It's the kind of action that can bring smiles to a rainy night when you'd rather be swimming, coziness to a fretful baby who'd rather be snoozing.

It's a journey. There are storms of wrong decisions. Muck of poor responses. And sunshine of good choices. The sunshine, perhaps better spelled SONshine, is where we must focus. We choose with each event to show Christlike care and encourage it in our children—no matter how we feel. We value our children and treat them with the same respect we know any fellow believer deserves. Jesus himself said, "Whatever you did for one of the least of these brothers of mine, you did for me" (Matthew 25:40).

Keep On Choosing

When we arrived at the hotel on our way home from D.C., I wasn't in the mood to cheerfully go supper-hunting. But I acted my way into a new feeling. God describes this process in Romans 12:1a: "Offer your bodies as living sacrifices, holy and pleasing to God." As we choose to honor God with tiny but significant enjoying and equipping actions, we complete a "spiritual act of worship" (Romans 12:1b). It's just as holy as attending church, perhaps more so, because it's worship in real life. Enjoyment is a habit we grow and actions we choose—day by precious day.

Enjoyment is living out the Psalmist's prayer: "May the words of my mouth and the meditation of my heart be pleasing in your sight, O Lord, my Rock and my Redeemer" (Psalm 19:14). We please God with caring words about and caring attitudes toward our children. He smiles when those words and attitudes ring out through our whole household. And as our children hear these words, they turn toward the Rock, the only One able to give them the security and power to face whatever life sends their way. Joyful days are a dream, certainly. But they become possible because of God's power (Philippians 4:13).

I didn't master enjoyment in that one simple choice prompted by my friend nor on that single road trip. I faced a new decision that very next day, one that meant demonstrating how to have fun as a family yet respect people and rules. After a peaceful night's sleep in our hotel room, we awoke to find the rain had stopped. "We can swim! We can swim!" the girls exclaimed.

There was one small problem. The pool didn't open until 10:00. We'd be three hours down the road by then. I pondered whether to sneak into the pool and swim quietly or ask permission first. The former meant we might be asked to leave the pool. The latter meant we risked being told no. More importantly, not to ask meant being dishonest.

I decided to call the front desk for permission to swim. I explained that my children had wanted to swim the night before but we had gotten in late and it had rained. I said we would have to leave before the pool opened and wondered if we could swim for a short while if we were absolutely quiet. The woman said, "Certainly. Just be very quiet. Thanks for asking."

Her warm response prompted me to thank God. I didn't yet realize how very right God's guidance had been.

"The pool doesn't open for another three hours," I explained to the girls. "Because some people like to sleep late in hotels, we must be absolutely quiet. Do you think you can swim silently?"

"Oh yes, we can do that," they said, beginning to slip into their swimming suits.

"I think you can too," I encouraged them. "But if either of you says a word you'll both have to leave the pool."

"We'll be quiet," they promised, putting on their flip-flops.

At the bottom of the elevator we discovered that the pool entrance was well within view of the breakfast lobby. Our deed would be obvious not only to hotel personnel but to a lobby full of donut-eating guests.

> As we choose to honor God with tiny but significant enjoying and equipping actions, we complete a "spiritual act of worship" (Romans 12:1b).

The woman at the desk waved as we went by. I thanked God once again for His nudge to be open rather than sneaky. One of the guests flashed us a huge smile. We shortly found out why—the water was subzero! The first plunge almost spurted a shout right out of the girls.

"Whoa! It's freezing," Sarah whispered with ice on her breath.

"But it's okay! We don't mind," Emily quickly added, with a smile from ear to ear.

Our swim lasted a total of seven minutes. Yet it's their favorite set of photos from our trip. "You should have felt that water! Like swimming in ice cubes!" they comment.

Children already know the rightness of enjoyment. They see the fun of water rather than the discomfort of arctic cold. They savor the spontaneity rather than worry about how long they'll have.

"Thanks, God, for teaching me through my children," I inwardly prayed.

In wet swimming suits and amid the smiles of amused onlookers, we grabbed a few donuts and returned to our room to change clothes. Armed with rotating jawbreakers, we started, rested and fresh, on the last ten hours of our trip. We entered the highway and one by one began to giggle. There was the McDonald's. Three miles down the road, at the next exit. We discovered a previously unknown but now most essential truth that in some parts of the country lodging exits are separate from food exits.

"I guess we were on the right road after all last night," I suggested, beginning to worry that I'd made the wrong choice by turning around.

"But we wouldn't have found our jawbreakers!" said Sarah, relieved that we *hadn't* found the McDonald's.

God did it again. Through the eyes of my children He taught me that life is meant to be enjoyed even when it doesn't go as we want it to. He taught me through a couple of silly jawbreakers, and an imperfect night that became ever-so-perfect.

Joy Tip

Perfect days come along once every million years or so. We can take the days we have and enjoy them, or we can waste away our days with fretting and feuding. We don't have the option of trading these days for better ones. We do have the option of calling on God's power and then delighting in the surprises He brings.

2

GET OUTTA MY FACE!

"Love your neighbor as yourself." If you keep on biting and devouring each other, watch out or you will be destroyed by each other.

—Galatians 5:14–15

"She's looking at me!"

"Tell her to stop interrupting my homework and I'll stop looking at her."

"I'm not interrupting! You asked me a question!"

"But the conversation's over now."

"You're just mad because you have more homework than me."

"Yes, I am mad. And it's going to get worse if you don't leave me alone!"

"Well if I had something to do, I wouldn't be hanging around you!"

It was one of those days. Anna had too much homework, Beth too little homework. Beth was restless, Anna stressed. Each wanted the other's attention, but for different reasons. Beth wanted company; Anna wanted sympathy.

None of the usual tension-busting tactics had worked. Their father, Barry, had offered new crafts and new books to Beth to keep her busy. He'd offered breaks and encouragement to Anna to keep her on task. He'd reminded Beth that Anna was busy, reminded Anna that Beth was restless, and reminded himself to stay calm. He had prompted each to understand and meet the needs of the other. But still they bickered. If Anna gave Beth an idea, Beth was bored with it. If Beth gave Anna support, Anna accused her of interrupting.

When Anna said blue, Beth said red. If Beth said yes, Anna said no. It was one of those "terrible-horrible-no-good-very-bad days."

An afternoon of picky bickering and endless whining is enough to tempt even the most loving of us to be short-tempered, and to forget all about building a family where people actually like one another. "Lord, give me strength," Barry prayed, conscious that yelling is a big temptation for him. He thanked God for helping him think before he spoke. He pushed his mind to understand the reasons for his daughters' behavior.

Reason 1: They were tired. It had been a busy week with little time to relax with their favorite pursuits.

Reason 2: They were hungry. It was near suppertime and all three of them were famished.

Reason 3: They had miles to go before either rest or food. Anna had homework and Barry was hurrying to finish the late-day tasks. Both he and Anna wanted to finish before sitting down to eat.

Reason 4: Some days are just like that.

But none of the reasons excused their picking and fussing. *Why are they so childish?* Barry lamented.

Beth and Anna act childishly because they're children with limited experience and perspective. But there's more to it than that. Beth and Anna act childishly because they're human. In the eternal scheme of things, we adults aren't that much more mature than our children. We all get in bad moods and we don't like people in our face when we feel grouchy. We'd rather whine about our to-do list than complete it. We don't want to travel long distances, sleep on an unfamiliar bed, or be kissed by the too-huggish aunt. We avoid shots, doctor visits, and unpleasant news.

But we're the adults. So we must be the catalysts for Christlikeness in the midst of any circumstance, even the grumpy ones. We parents must show our children how to respond in ways that show care, whether the mood is calm or chaotic, kind or caustic. Together with God, we can show our children how to solve the problem rather than make it worse, how to ease the conflict rather than escalate it.

Notice the Need

OK, God, Barry prayed, humbled by the task before him. *Give me words.*

"Girls, you've been bickering ever since I picked you up from school. I'm not sure what the problem is—"

"The problem is I have homework, and she doesn't," said Anna.

"The problem is she keeps fussing at me," said Beth.

"Well, maybe I do know the problem," Barry agreed. "But I don't know why it's affecting you this way. We've had other big homework days without this impact. Maybe it's late in the week and we're all tired."

> No child is always happy or cooperative. And in the eternal scheme of things, we parents aren't that much different.

"I'm exhausted," said Anna. "But I'll never get to bed if I don't finish this homework."

"And you'll never finish if you don't quit bugging me," added Beth with less than pure motives.

"Okay, girls!" Barry said with more volume than he intended. *Calm me, Lord. I'm getting pulled into bicker-mode.* With God-given calmness Barry added, "Beth, we've tried all the things you usually enjoy doing—crafts, books, computer time. You're going to have to find something interesting to do that doesn't irritate Anna."

"Yeah, Beth!" agreed Anna.

"And, Anna, you're going to have to move to a place where you won't be so easily interrupted. I know you like to study in the middle of the den, but Beth does have to walk through there," Barry said.

"No she doesn't. She can stay in one room," insisted Anna.

"She could, but I'm trying to be fair to both of you," Barry insisted. "I think the best thing would be to spend an hour in your rooms. It's not punishment. It's giving each other opportunity to do what needs doing. You could study, Anna. And, Beth, you could read or work on your hook rug."

"But I don't want to move to my room," said Anna. "I'm already spread out here."

"I'll help you move your stuff," Barry said. "Then in an hour you can come back out, ready to get along. If you can't get along, right back to your rooms you'll go."

"Tell her to quit interrupting and we'll get along fine," said Anna.

"Tell her to quit accusing me and there won't be a problem," said Beth.

"It's a two-way street. Beth, you need to treat Anna's study time with quiet and without interruptions," Barry agreed. "But at the same time, Anna, you have to decide to let Beth walk through the room without accusations."

"Yeah," said Beth, feeling vindicated.

"Whoa," Barry said. "See, you're already fighting about who fights. Let's all grab a piece of cheese, because hunger might be part of the problem. Then move to your rooms and I'll see you in an hour. If you come out before then, you'll get an extra thirty minutes."

"What if Beth comes out and I don't?" asked Anna.

"She'll get the extra thirty minutes and you won't," Barry said, trying to stay fair. "Now look at your watches. Do you have 4:28?"

"Yes," said Beth.

"No," said Anna. "I'm 4:25 because the clocks at school are fast."

"Beth come out at 5:28 by your watch; Anna, come out at 5:25 by your watch, 5:28 by the clock in your rooms. Then we'll work together to design some ways to get along."

Enjoying life with our children doesn't mean constant company with no privacy. Sometimes it means time apart. Sometimes it means enforcing peace. The words "enforce" and "peace" don't seem to go together. They're like "legislate morality." In the "heart sense" you can neither legislate morality nor enforce peace. But in the "action sense," you can. When Mom fines her children for saying critical words, they tend to talk things out calmly. When Dad takes away his son's baseball equipment because he cheats in the game, he tends to play fair next time. When Barry hugs his daughters for studying co-operatively, they tend to repeat that harmony.

Enforced peace begins with actions only. But heart commitment follows, especially when we explain the reasons for our enforcement: "You two can study in the same room if you'll cooperate. But if you bully and pick at each other, you'll hurt each other and accomplish nothing. I don't want that, and God doesn't want that. So I'll separate you if that happens."

Show Them How

Why do we parents have to help our kids learn to get along? Because neither they nor we were born knowing how—we all must

WONDER ACTIONS

It often takes only simple actions to help children enjoy each other and parents enjoy their children:

Reward kind behavior: Kids do what they get attention for. So notice when they say "Nice try!" rather than "Dumb move!" Praise them when they listen to each other or play a game cooperatively. Hug them for including each other rather than banning each other.

Go by shoelace length: When taking turns, the youngest gets tired of always being last, or the oldest gets tired of always letting the younger one go first. So go by hair color, then alphabetically by first name, then by shoelace length, and so on. Encourage your children to find more fun-and-fair ways to decide who goes first.

Give time apart: Privacy isn't punishment. Provide a consistent time alone each day. This energizes each family member to cooperate. Options include a private spot for homework, an hour to read, uninterrupted time in the tree house, dinner out with Dad on Thursdays.

Time turns: "We only have two bicycles, so you two ride the bikes for ten minutes and then the other two can ride. We'll use this timer to keep it fair."

Count and divide: "There are six chocolates so we can each have two," or "There's only one piece of pie left. Let's cut it into thirds."

Work it out ahead of time: "We need to finish four showers in the next hour to make it to the play on time. That gives you fifteen minutes apiece. If you take more than fifteen minutes, what should we do?" To boost their cooperation, let children decide the consequences. Besides that, they often think of more creative solutions than we adults ever would: "At the fifteen-minute mark, you come out of the shower, no matter how soapy you are."

learn through experience. Babies want what they want when they want it. They cry to get food or company. But quite rapidly they learn to stop crying and give grins in return for that company. They learn to delay their hunger to give one more coo. Why? Grinning and cooing win attention. Grinning and cooing have the even better side effects of showing affection for the givers of that attention. Isn't it neat that God has created love to reward both the giver and the receiver?

The first impulse of toddlers is to throw tantrums when they want something. But when those tantrums go unrewarded, toddlers learn to ask calmly and wait patiently for what they want. School-age children prefer the biggest piece or the longest turn. But when they discover that cutting the brownie pan into equal portions gives everybody the biggest possible piece, they enjoy making others happy. Teenagers like to tell every detail of the movie they watched. But as they feel the frustration of being interrupted, they learn to listen as much as they talk.

It's a journey of maturity, of moving from self-centeredness to other-centeredness. It's discovering that God is as interested in the way we treat each other as in how much we read the Bible. It's learning to love—and to enjoy. Along this road, we discover that the only way to find happiness is to give it to others: "Each of you should look not only to your own interests, but also to the interests of others" (Philippians 2:4).

Does this maturing process happen automatically? Of course not. We all know church leaders who still throw tantrums to get what they want. We watch old-enough-to-know-better children sneak a second turn before the others have a first. We lament over fifty-year-old teenagers who still try to prove themselves with daredevil stunts and exaggerated stories.

Our children won't automatically become loving. In fact, they'll stay focused on themselves unless we prod them to care for others.

The Holy Spirit does the transformation, but we parents make it easier for our children to see, understand, and heed His work. As we show them how to value God and each other, they find the joy they're looking for. They discover that the sweetness of sharing is richer than the sweetness of the biggest brownie hogged and eaten alone.

Save the Hassle

It's easy to applaud the idea of children living peaceably together. It's even easy to commit to helping it happen. But it's not so easy when my toddler throws a tantrum in a busy grocery store aisle or in front of a friend whose children are perfectly behaved. I'll do almost anything to get her quiet. One little candy bar won't hurt just this time, will it?

Yes.

Because next time she'll do it again—only louder—because it worked so well the first time. It will definitely hurt *me* to let my beloved child make a complete fool of herself in front of staring onlookers. But it will hurt *her* more to be embarrassed again and again, to be out of control and terrified because she doesn't know how to reign in her wild feelings.

Many parents refuse to teach their children to handle their difficulties, preferring that their kids just be good. Or they let someone else handle that part. It's too much hassle, they reason. But when we don't teach our children to love, they will "bite and devour each other" (Galatians 5:15).

It is a hassle. It takes energy and courage to enforce peace. It takes inventiveness and preparation to guide a room full of children to enjoy each other's company rather than compete at who can be the meanest. It's not easy to provide the boundaries and structure that make it more likely our children will choose to be fair and considerate. Here's the good news: we need not muster any of this by ourselves. In Philippians 4:19, God has promised to meet all our needs. He'll give us the energy, courage, ideas, words, and structure to guide our children to build closeness rather than factions. We simply provide the commitment and the go-ahead to do as God bids.

And the best news is that all this *saves* hassle in the long run. When I let my toddler throw one tantrum without responding, I save the hassle of a thousand more tantrums.

For your children's sake, help them "love [their] neighbor as [themselves]" (Galatians 5:14). Show them how to become caring citizens of the kingdom of Jesus Christ. As they treat each other the way they want to be treated, they have the power to enjoy each other. They can find solutions that make them both happy, rather than fight to the finish. They can build a personality that invites others to choose them as friends.

It's not all hassle. We also have the privilege of applauding our children when they choose to get along, when they work together to create happiness: "Let's break all these pieces of chalk in half and then we can both have all the colors at once!" agreed Barry's daughters one morning after bickering that the other took too long with the best colors of chalk.

They found their own solution to a tough problem. And Barry nearly burst with pride.

Notice Your Similarities

Kids aren't the only ones who have a bicker-mode. We parents fall into the same trap. Barry's family had awaited a happy day for weeks: Beth would compete in a regional spelling bee ten hours from home. She was ecstatic and had been counting the days, then the hours. Barry and the girls left early, singing and giddy and excited. Anna quizzed Beth on spelling words as they drove. Beth quizzed Anna on the test she'd have when they returned home. All three enjoyed car snacks and a picnic. It was a delightful trip.

They arrived at the hotel long after their usual bedtime. Barry knew Beth needed rest to do her best. So he was eager to get both girls into bed. He planned to send Beth to the shower first, but Anna assured him she could get in and out in three minutes. That would give Beth time to unpack her pajamas and prepare for the next day. Three minutes stretched to thirteen, and Barry feared they would extend to thirty. It was Beth's day and she was the one who needed more rest.

"C'mon, Anna! You've got to get out to give Beth time to get her shower. You said you'd be out in three minutes!"

"I couldn't help it that the hotel shower didn't heat up as fast as at home. Just be patient, Dad," she urged.

"We don't have time tonight. You've got to go faster," Barry urged back.

"I will, I will," she promised.

Five more minutes. Barry knocked at the door to say Anna needed to move out. She could finish her beauty routine in the hotel room mirror.

That didn't go over well. But Barry made Anna leave the bathroom anyway. To make matters worse, the bathtub drain got stuck.

WONDER WORDS

The best way for children to live peacefully with each other is through choosing to be kind. But let's be realistic: sometimes they need a little external motivation. Words such as these give the reason for the choice and help children love their neighbor as themselves (Galatians 5:14):

- "You were very thoughtful to invite Lee to play. That's loving like Jesus loves."

- "I think you could have been a little calmer during your disagreement with Luke. He was just asking a question. What might you have said to make things kinder?"

- "Since both of you want the icing rose, let's cut it right down the middle."

- "When you do all the talking, you force everyone to focus on you and make them feel like their ideas don't matter. Take turns telling stories so everybody feels important."

- "When you don't say anything, people might think you're not interested in them. Overcome your shyness to comment and compliment. God will help you."

- "When you lie, nobody wants to be around you. They assume they can't trust you. Tell the truth no matter how hard it is."

- "Be sure to compliment Nina on her good grade. Friends show happiness for each other."

Several long minutes later Beth started her shower. Barry helped her wash her hair and then returned to the hotel room to find that instead of combing out her hair, Anna had sat on the bed and sulked.

"Oh, Anna, you're supposed to be in bed by now! Please get ready!"

What was wrong with his usually responsible girls? What was he going to do now? He had one angry daughter who wasn't about to budge from the bed. He had another who was casually combing her hair in the bathroom—the one who was prone to headaches if she didn't get enough rest. *Maybe it's my fault*, thought Barry. *Maybe I'm not being fair. Since Anna and Beth are acting differently than usual, that might be it.*

So Barry pulled Beth from the bathroom and sent Anna back in to finish her beauty treatment.

That didn't go over well either. Beth was so irate about being pulled from the steamy warm bathroom into the chilly hotel room that she went to sleep without letting Barry kiss her good-night. Her anger made sense; Barry had been too sudden. But he didn't know what to do about it now.

Anna finally came back out of the bathroom with her hair combed. But she was stonily silent.

What am I doing? wondered Barry. *We waited so long for today. It was supposed to be perfect.*

He apologized to Anna. He kissed his now sleeping Beth. Barry stayed awake long after he heard the soft snoozing of his children. He regretted, and relived, and pondered how he could have made the evening go more smoothly. He could have communicated better up front. He could have set a timer and said they had a set amount of time and that was it. He could have put Beth in first, since she took faster showers and needed more rest. He could have sat down with the girls before showers, acknowledged that everyone was tired, and mapped out a shower strategy.

That all sounded good, but Barry had already blown it. Everybody was asleep and he couldn't start over. He wondered if either girl would sleep well now that they'd had such a stormy evening. But he couldn't wake them to ask. That would be meeting Barry's need, not theirs. The only thing left to do was to decide what to do in the morning. And Barry needed sleep so he wouldn't repeat the same sleepy scenario the next day.

After a restless night, he apologized again and asked for a fresh start. He told the girls they had fifty-five minutes to get ready, that they would have to leave at that point no matter what hair was out of place or what sock still felt twisted. They would need to work together to make it, and if they finished a little early they'd have time for donuts in the lobby. He asked for ideas on how to get ready without getting in each other's way. He asked the girls if they thought they could do it.

They agreed that they could. And they did.

The new day helped. The refreshed-by-sleep minds helped. The repentant Barry helped. The donuts in the lobby helped. Barry and his girls made it early to the competition—spiffed up, clear-thinking, and ready to cheer Beth on.

Like Barry, we parents still have a lot to learn about getting along with our families. Like our children, we get tired and let our grouchiness lead to attacks rather than solutions. We make big mistakes even during the happiest times. Showing our children how to enjoy life during disagreement includes modeling what to do when we blow it. It includes recognizing when we feel anxious or worn out, so we can give extra attention to patience and cooperation.

Under ideal circumstances, we can alert family members when we're feeling grouchy and go to our rooms for a nap or a bit of privacy. But most of the time we don't have that luxury. We've got to muster up the last bit of patience at the bottom of our reserves. And we ask God for power to stay kind.

Life isn't easy. Circumstances can make tempers fly. But by the grace of God we can treat each other with kindness and respect. It's not that much easier for us adults than for children. But it's crucial for both.

Filter the Hurt

We needn't feel badly when our children disagree with each other. It's the *way* they disagree that counts. Disagreement between two people is as natural as the sun rising in the morning. But like the sun, disagreement can do some heavy-duty damage if not handled properly. The sun warms when the angle is right, but it burns when it's directly overhead. Disagree with care, rather than burn each other with caustic criticism and one-upmanship. All family members get burned when one sibling (or parent) insists on her way at the expense of others.

The sun works even when it's behind a cloud. Similarly, disagreements can help both children grow if viewpoints are expressed thoughtfully and heard with genuine interest. Perspective is the name of the game. When we put ourselves in the other's shoes, we can understand why they feel and act as they do. Heather Whitestone, dedicated Christian and Miss America 1995, tells this story of perspective:

I hold up a quarter and ask, "What do you see?"

"A head," you answer.

"No. It's an eagle," I respond,

"It's a head!" you insist.

"Eagle!"

"Head!"

"Eagle!"

"Head!"

> It takes energy and courage to enforce peace and to live it ourselves.

"Can't you see it's an eagle!"

Finally you ask me, "What makes you say 'eagle'?"

I turn around the quarter and show you the eagle.

"Oh, I understand!" you say. "It's different on your side."

"And I see the head on your side."

We can then agree that we both see a quarter.

This is perspective: two sides of the same coin, two real needs by two real people in one space in time. With perspective we can understand the feelings and ideas of the other person. We can find harmony even when we initially need two different things. We care the way we'd like to be cared about.

Anna may insist that it's not fair that Beth get a free afternoon. Beth may insist that it's no fun to have Anna doing homework when she wants to play. But both need attention. Anna needs help with her homework, and Beth needs help finding something interesting to do independently. As each sees the other's perspective, they help each other. They can achieve Christlike harmony even during chaos.

"Beth, I've got tons of homework. Please don't come in here singing about being bored. I'd love to have your problem right now!" explained Anna, momentarily putting aside her pressured feelings to recognize Beth's point of view.

Putting herself in Anna's shoes, Beth thinks, *If I were Anna I'd be pretty jealous of me. I'll get her a glass of cold water to help her study better. Then I'll snuggle up with a book in the other room. If I stay still maybe she can study better.*

"I'm sorry I sang," Beth said. "I am bored, but it doesn't help you to tell you that. Do you want some ice water before I go off to read?"

Yeah, right. I've never seen siblings act this way.

Certainly it's a tall order for two young girls to get along when they're feeling irritable. But it's also a tall order for two grown adults. It's not human nature to get along. None of us naturally sees and responds to the other's point of view, unless it's to our advantage. It takes supernatural power to do something like that. Yet this is exactly what I'm recommending—call on God's supernatural power to help you see the other's point of view. As you see, you can understand. As you understand, you can respond. And as you respond, you build harmony rather than discord. It's a dream, all right, but one worth pursuing. God himself recommends it:

"You, my brothers, were called to be free. But do not use your freedom to indulge the sinful nature; rather, serve one another in love. The entire law is summed up in a single command: 'Love your neighbor as yourself.' If you keep on biting and devouring each other, watch out or you will be destroyed by each other" (Galatians 5:13–15).

> Certainly it's a tall order for two young girls to get along when they're feeling irritable. But it's also a tall order for two grown adults. Yet this is exactly what I'm recommending—call on God's supernatural power to help you see the other's point of view.

Grow the Harmony

Anna and Beth didn't want to destroy each other, but once they got into the argument they might have. Beth just wanted to give her frustration away. Anna just wanted to lighten her load. Anna wanted her way. Beth wanted hers. There's nothing wrong with these feelings, but there's something wrong with selfishly taking your feelings out on each other. The natural way is the self-centered way—you do it my way on my timing and at my convenience.

The spiritual way is the cooperative way—let's tell each other what we need, understand, and then work together to solve both problems. Let's see each other's perspective and work to see both sides of the quarter. This way not only works, it makes people happy. And this harmony pleases God.

No two people will always be kind. But any two people can work to become kinder with each conversation. As we parents model how to disagree and remain kind, our children model our actions. As we show our children how the other might be feeling, our children learn to see and heed each other's perspective. As we discover together with our children the words and tones that show love in the midst of struggle, we honor Jesus Christ.

No child is too young or old, too handicapped or gifted, too talkative or quiet to contribute to family joy. But every child must learn how to do so. It won't happen on its own. But it will happen as we parents become students of God and nurture our children as God directs us. Our children then bloom. They deliver love, joy, peace, patience, kindness, goodness, faithfulness, gentleness, and self control as we do the same (Galatians 5:22–23).

Joy Tip

All children fuss, whine, get moody, and argue. Enjoying life as a family means showing our children how to overcome bad moods to show real love for each other.

3

WILL THEY LIVE HAPPILY EVER AFTER?

*Being confident of this, that he who began a good work in you
will carry it on to completion until the day of Christ Jesus.*

—Philippians 1:6

"Just give him to the Lord," I heard the speaker say about a wayward child who had made choices that were destroying him and others.

Partly true, I thought. *But that's an easy excuse to sit back and do
nothing.* God gave our children to us and they can't raise themselves.
We can't wash our hands of them. If *we* don't give our children what
they need to grow joy, no one will. So let's determine to work hand
in hand with God to show our sons and daughters how to love God,
how to love others, and how to love themselves (Matthew 22:36–40).

What our children learn as they grow up with us reaches far beyond the walls of our homes. The way a child's family life impacts
the rest of his or her life is, in fact, a great motivator to work at
valuing our children. Let me explain how two families worked to
shape two toddlers—and how their determination played out as
those two children grew to love each other.

Friends since childhood, Tyrone and Meredith were each glad to
see a familiar face on their first fearsome days of high school. During
their freshman and sophomore years, they said hellos and chatted
once or twice a week. As juniors, Meredith found herself disappointed if she didn't see Tyrone during the day. When Tyrone felt
like sharing good news, it was Meredith who came to mind. So they
found ways to be together without really dating. They hung around

after church just to talk. On school days, Tyrone always showed up at Meredith's locker before classes so they could tell each other what was coming that day. Meredith met him at his locker at the end of the day to hear how things had gone.

Tyrone loved Meredith's probing nature. She continually wanted to know how and why. Her questions made him think about why things happen the way they do, and how Christians should respond to—or cause—the events around them. She showed him that God was an integral part of every day, not just Sundays. Tyrone couldn't help but be excited about each day when he saw it through Meredith's eyes.

Meredith loved Tyrone's stories. He added such engaging detail to the simplest of events. Through his stories Meredith saw the feelings, hopes, dreams, and ideas behind the people in his stories—friends, family, strangers. His insight helped her overcome her habit of verbally slamming people. To Tyrone, each person was a unique individual with rare, defining characteristics. And when Meredith was around him, she couldn't help but see them the same way. How could she put down someone who was wonderfully one of a kind, someone who mattered to God and to Tyrone?

Tyrone saw people. Meredith saw events. Each took life as a continuous adventure—always something to see, to understand, to explore. Together they helped each other grasp the wonder in both the happy and the sad, the simple and the complex.

Eventually they needed more time together than the before-and-afters. So Tyrone offered to cook supper for Meredith one Friday night. "We can walk to the ice cream shop afterward for dessert," he added. "It's a long walk, but it will give us a chance to talk."

"I'd like that a lot," Meredith responded. "I love long walks." His date offer was creative. She was delighted. She looked forward to talking—to conversation time they wouldn't get if they had a standard out-to-dinner-and-a-movie date.

———

What prepared Tyrone and Meredith for such natural growth from friendship to romance? What helped them find ease rather than anxiousness in being together? *Their families gave them the tools to build good relationships.* Then they showed them how to sharpen and use each love-building tool. They began with these:

T *enacity*
O *utward faithfulness*
O *h!*
L *aughter*
S *peaking skills*

Provide Quality Tools

Tenacity

Determination and perseverance matter in almost every pursuit of life. This stick-to-it-iveness is what gets done what needs doing. Meredith had it as a two-year-old. When the glittering vase was too high to reach, she pushed a chair over to the counter. Because the chair was too high, she carried a box to it and then climbed from the box to the chair to the counter top. Once on the counter, she ran her fingers over the vase to find out where the sparkle came from. Because she couldn't touch the twinkle with her fingers, she picked up a second vase to tap the sparkling spots. She didn't mean for the vases to crack; she just wanted to know what made the first one glimmer.

The tenacity of a toddler has its weaknesses—it can cause damage. But tenacity itself is good. It will enable Meredith to move past any obstacle to hold to her Christian conviction, to choose the thoughtful action, to overcome powerful wrong. Meredith's parents preserved this good by teaching young Meredith to pair cherishing with investigation. "Mama's vase is special to her. If you want to see it, tell us and we'll bring it down for you. That will let you see it, but not hurt the vase or you. You could fall from the counter."

"I won't fall. I'm careful," Meredith insisted.

"We know you're careful, but falls can happen anyway. Let's keep both feet on the ground."

Speaking and enforcing these guidelines let Meredith keep her tenacity while preventing the hurt. She grew to understand why mama's special things mattered to her and asked mama to hold them while she touched. To reward Meredith's compassion, her mother was careful to answer Meredith's questions or show her how to investigate in ways that would give her answers: "The sparkle comes from glitter under a layer of glaze. Here, I'll show you. Paint a bit of this Christmas ball with clear nail polish. Now shake glitter on it while the polish is wet. When that dries a little, cover it with another layer of clear polish. Now, it's been five minutes. Touch it. See? You can't feel the glitter but it's inside there."

As a thirty-two-year-old, Meredith's tenacity has kept her probing to discover what makes healthy cells sparkle in the place of cancer cells. She's after a cure for cancer, and she won't stop until she finds it. Perhaps she'll be the one who discovers a way to prompt the human immune system to squash cancer permanently. Her commitment may just result in curing the disease that attacks one in three persons.

Outward faithfulness

We might call this tool integrity or honesty. It's the personality quality that prompts children to live their faith rather than just claim it. Tyrone learned about outward faithfulness—or the lack of it—from his friend Alex. Alex called himself a faithful Christian, but he had one little problem. He lied. He didn't really mean to lie; he just didn't want to hurt anyone's feelings. One night Alex and Tyrone were supposed to lead a large Bible study together. Alex couldn't bear to see the disappointed look in Tyrone's eyes when he said, "I'd like to be there, but I can't." So he just didn't say it. Alex avoided seeing the disappointment, but he also never saw the hurt he inflicted—the confusion, then sheer panic in Tyrone's face when he was left to lead the entire Bible study. Alex never saw Tyrone struggle to lead with only half the resources, frantically trying to fill in where Alex was supposed to teach. But Alex did see the anger in Tyrone's eyes when he encountered him the next day. "Where were you?" Tyrone said with aggravation. "You said you'd be there." Alex felt bad. He really did. But he thought his way was easier.

Alex found an easy way to slip into youth conferences without paying. He discovered that everybody registered that first day and then came and went with registration badges. Nobody really checked the badges—so Alex just came in with a crowd. If anybody asked, he said he forgot his badge. *It doesn't cost them any more for me to be here. And I'm not hurting anybody. Besides, this is a Christian conference and I'm learning more about God. Last night's session was great!* Uplifting for Alex, but what about Tyrone, who saved for months to go? How would he feel knowing Alex had freeloaded and driven the price up for him?

Alex liked to make everybody feel good, so once when he went out with a crowd he told the waitress it was Will's birthday. The waitress returned with a free birthday cake and a big gang from the kitchen to sing a boisterous birthday song. Will was so caught by surprise that he didn't say anything. He knew it wasn't his birthday but he didn't want to put Alex on the spot. Tyrone was even more uncomfortable watching. Alex looked pleased with himself. He thought he'd made Will happy. But Will wanted to crawl under the table. When the waitress left, Alex whispered to Tyrone, "That cake didn't cost much. Besides, it was funny. What this restaurant doesn't know won't hurt them."

Easier. Money saving. What they don't know won't hurt them. Tyrone had heard all that before. It sounded good. But there was one problem. It wasn't true. The first lie left Tyrone hung out to dry. The second stole from other conference-goers. The third embarrassed Will and cheated a restaurant.

With each lie, Tyrone became more committed to truth. He recognized why the Bible says, "The truth will set you free" (John 8:32).

Oh!

This third tool is an attitude of discovery, a quest for understanding, an openness to learning how. Four-year-old Meredith had it.

"How many gons are there?" she asked her dad one day.

"Gons?"

"Yeah. You know, hexa-gons, penta-gons. How many are there?"

"Well there are pentagons with five sides, hexagons with six, and octagons with eight. Heptagons or septagons might be the names for seven-sided figures, and nonagons have nine sides. There are probably more, but that's all I know."

"Oh. What about three-sided figures?"

"Those are called triangles."

"Why not three-agons or trio-agons?"

"I don't know, but those would be good names."

"How about two-sided or four-sided or one-sided?"

"One-sided figures are called lines, two-sided are called angles, and four-sided are called squares."

"Why aren't they all gons?"

"Well, maybe for variety, maybe because the namers liked the names 'triangle' and 'line.' What do you think?"

"I think it might have been better to have all gons. But I like the name 'line.' Who were the namers?"

Young Meredith is in "oh!-mode," a time of delicious discovery. Her curiosity and openness to new understanding will later inspire her to understand why her friend won't talk, or why her husband acts crossly, or why her child is so ecstatic. Rather than presume her friend is mad, she'll ask what's wrong. When she discovers that her friend's grandfather died, she'll listen as he tells her about it. Rather than accuse her husband of being a grump, she'll invite him to tell her why he's not himself. When he explains he has a sore throat and is worried that he won't have a voice for tomorrow's presentation, she'll fix him hot lemonade to soothe his throat. Rather than declare her son "hyper," she'll ask, "What has you so excited?" She'll join his dance when he tells her he finally made a 100 on a spelling test.

> Spirituality is showing love when you feel like attacking, joy when you'd rather whine, peace when you'd rather argue, patience when you'd rather demand, kindness when you'd rather be cruel.

Because none of us knows as much as all of us, and because God has given us a world where there's always more to learn, an eagerness for learning is crucial. Discovery is the opposite of know-it-all-ness, the opposite of pride, the opposite of I-don't-need-any-help-from-anybody. It's the biblical quality of humility, of teachableness, of growth. It's a strong quality that shows real maturity. It will free adult Meredith and adult Tyrone to get along, to work out misunderstandings, to truly enjoy each other. Discovery grows into wisdom—the ability to live for Jesus in everyday life. Like Meredith's dad, prompt your children's "Oh!" by applauding questions. Highlight their insights and patiently answer the 437 questions the average four-year-old asks every day.

Laughter

Laughter is the delight of love. But it's not as easy as it sounds. Too many of us laugh *at* each other rather than *with* each other. Tyrone's grandfather knows the secret to true laughter. His tales are always true, and always make the child feel truly cherished. He tells of Tyrone learning to read:

"He was just a little fellow, maybe three or four. He begged to go along with me wherever I went. And that was fine with me. I loved taking him because he eagerly helped in whatever way I asked. He wanted to know every detail about how and why I did what I did. One morning we went to the hardware store to get paint for the back porch. It was to be his first time there. We talked all during breakfast about going to the hardware store as soon as we finished eating. I told him about the interesting bins of bolts, about the nice people who liked to help, about the paints in endless colors. He could hardly eat he was so excited.

"When we arrived he looked around eagerly: 'Here are the bins you told me about!' 'There are the helpers you told me about!' 'Here are the paint cans!' Suddenly, excited as could be, he looked at the wall and said, 'Oh Grandpa! I know just what that sign says!'

"What does it say, Tyrone?" I asked.

" 'It says P-A-I-N-T . . . H-H-Hardware Store!'

"He'd been watching children's programs about how to sound out letters to read words. He knew that 'hardware' started with a 'ha' sound, but didn't yet know how each letter sounded. So he figured the word on the wall had to say Hardware Store since that's where we were. Of course it said something else, but pretty good figuring, wouldn't you say?"

Tyrone's grandfather taught Tyrone the secret to storytelling and the secret to loving laughter. What is that secret? Always use words and stories and laughter to build up. The Bible describes it like this: "Let us consider how we may spur one another on toward love and good deeds . . . let us encourage one another—and all the more as you see the Day approaching" (Hebrews 10:24–25).

Tyrone's grandfather could have said, "The kid didn't even know the difference between a 'P' sound and an 'H' sound!" But that would have been the ultimate in cruelty. It would have turned laughter into mocking.

"Never use stories to criticize people or make them feel foolish," Tyrone's grandfather would say. "Caring laughter is the most uniting of people skills."

"Like our butter tradition," he continued. "When I was about your age I got butter smeared all over my thumb passing the butter around the family supper table. Titters of laughter from my brother, and then my mother suddenly exploded into hysterics. It really did end up being funny. Now all of us family members *try* to get butter on the other's thumb while passing the butter. Guests at the table wonder why everyone passes the butter plate flat-handed. Your Meredith discovered the reason when her thumb got intentionally buttered. It was a sign of acceptance, of initiation into our family. And now she's a flat-handed butter passer, too."

Speaking skills

As a young boy Tyrone talked too much. Like his grandfather, he was a confident storyteller. But unlike his grandfather he hadn't learned the fine art of dialogue, of listening as much as he talked. Tyrone assumed everyone wanted to hear every detail of his tales. In the process no one could get a word in edgewise. It wasn't that Tyrone said *bad* things—he said *all* the things. His grade school friends saw him as self-centered and braggish.

Young Meredith had the opposite problem. She spoke so little that friends wondered if she noticed them at all. Why wouldn't she talk? Did she hate them or something? What was she thinking? Did anything matter to her? In truth, Meredith was deeply interested in people. Her curiosity about "gons" carried over to people. She wanted to know everything about everyone and voraciously consumed every word her friends spoke. She thrived on their ideas and longed to share hers. She just didn't know how to put them into words. Her eyes gave a hint of her eagerness, but still she kept silent.

Both Tyrone and Meredith needed communication skills. Tyrone needed to express his eagerness not just through speaking but through listening, and not just through question-answering but through question-asking. Meredith needed to speak up as well as hear. Neither skill came easily to the other. Meredith broke into a cold sweat whenever she had to talk. Tyrone had to sit on his words, and his hands, to keep from talking. But conversation-by-conversation they learned the fine art of give-and-take, the loneliness-easing skill of people-relating. Meredith's mother gave her "lessons" to help her progress step by step:

- Smile at someone new today.
- Say hi to someone today.
- Now say hi to two people.
- Now say hi to someone you don't usually talk to.
- Now give a compliment.
- Now ask a question.
- Advance to a conversation of four sentences.
- Invite someone over.

And so on—until Meredith could carry on a comfortable conversation, complete with humor.

Tyrone's grandfather urged him to tell a single story, and then ask questions to get someone else to tell a story, counting up to fifty before saying anything else. (Tyrone's grandfather decided that Tyrone counted too fast for a simple count of 1 to 10.)

Today both Tyrone and Meredith are caring and cooperative communicators. They talk out problems and mutually share joys. They use both their words and their ears to show interest, one of the strongest forms of love.

Wear the Tool Belt

Spirituality is the tool belt on which Meredith's and Tyrone's parents helped them hang all five tools. They showed the connection between these practical relationship skills and their Christian faith.

What picture comes to mind when you think of spirituality? Talking in a holy-sounding voice? Wearing a nun's habit? Going to church all the time? None of these hit the essence of spirituality. Spirituality is honoring God in every word, action, and attitude. It's Meredith saying kind words even when she's in a grouchy mood. It's Tyrone playing fair in card games. It's Meredith listening as carefully to her brother's story as she wants him to listen to hers. It's Tyrone sharing the bathroom with his three sisters. It's Meredith choosing

FAMILY FUNNIES

Laughing with your kids is a powerful way to show you treasure them, that their victories and mistakes matter to you:

Laughing *with* your kids recalls funny things they did in a way that makes them feel treasured;	Laughing *at* your kids replays the past in a way that makes them feel criticized or belittled.
Laughing *with* your kids lightens the moment.	Laughing *at* your kids raises tensions.
Laughing *with* your kids is hearing and enjoying their stories;	Laughing *at* your kids is attacking or changing their stories.
Laughing *with* your kids makes them feel a part of the action;	Laughing *at* your kids makes them feel like minor league players in the major leagues.
Laughing *with* your kids assures them everyone makes mistakes;	Laughing *at* your kids convinces them they are stupid or incompetent.
Laughing *with* your kids helps them value every person;	Laughing *at* your kids encourages gossip and slander.
Laughing *with* your kids empowers them to face obstacles;	Laughing *at* your kids weakens them and pushes them to retreat.
Laughing *with* your kids prompts a "Tell that story again!";	Laughing *at* your kids elicits "Don't you dare tell that in front of anybody!"

to drive carefully so no one gets hurt.

Spirituality is both Tyrone and Meredith showing love when they feel like attacking, joy when they'd rather whine, peace when they'd rather argue, patience when they'd rather demand, kindness when they'd rather be cruel, goodness when they'd rather be selfish, faithfulness when they'd rather betray, self-control when they'd rather lose their temper. It's rejecting jealousy for security, rejecting discord for harmony, rejecting rage for calm conversation, rejecting self-indulgence to do what's best for others. All these love qualities come from Galatians 5:19–23, in the Bible.

Spirituality impacts every area of life, every single minute of every single day. From the time they were young children, Tyrone's parents and Meredith's parents urged them to find ways to live on this earth as Jesus did. When middle-school-aged Meredith first noticed her people-slamming habit, she elicited her mom's help:

"Mom, I've been trying to say caring things rather than laugh at people, but it's not working," she said.

"It's hard, isn't it?" her mother responded. "It's not easy to say caring things when cuts are mostly what you hear. Instead of feeling bad, take the challenge by the horns and decide to win."

"But I keep losing," countered Meredith.

"See it as a word war," suggested her mother. "Head cruel words off at the pass and deliberately substitute compliments."

"It *feels* like a war, alright," agreed Meredith.

"And you're not alone in that. Remember what Paul said in Romans 7 and 8? He talks about the battle to do right," said her mom.

"But how can I win?" persisted Meredith.

"The Bible describes it like changing clothes. Take off the ornery words and put on compassion and kindness," explained her mom. "Make a deliberate switch. When you're wearing compassion, you find it easier to feel people's feelings, to talk to and about them like you'd want to be talked about. The 'com' in compassion means 'with,' so compassion is to feel with other people."

"I can feel with people," said Meredith. "But I still say mean things."

"It takes tenacity," explained her mom. "When you were little, you didn't let anything stop you when you wanted to get at something. Use that same tenacity to learn to encourage. Before you say anything, stop and check out your words. Only let out the ones that are both true and kind."

"Tenacity?" asked Meredith.

"Stick-to-it-iveness, commitment, going for the long haul, being a distance runner, staying with it until you reach the goal," said her mom.

"That's enough examples, Mom. I get it," said Meredith. "But it's so hard!"

"I agree," said her mom. "But little worth doing is easy. You can do it because God promises the power."

By welcoming Meredith's questions and by teaching without condemning, Meredith's mom equipped Meredith to be spiritual in the words she spoke every day. She prompted Meredith to use her tenacity to crack a persistent habit. Spirituality freed her to do what she really wanted to do—grow trusting friendships.

Build Houses of Love

As moms, dads, and grandparents taught love tools to Tyrone and Meredith, they didn't allow the tools to be kept in the garage. They insisted that Tyrone and Meredith use their tools daily to build joy, happiness, goodness, and family-feeling. Tyrone's *outward spirituality* got nicked up a bit when it came to being patient with his younger sister. Meredith's *speaking skills* needed refurbishing from time to time. But the more they used the tools the sharper they became. And their tools didn't rust when actively used to build houses of love.

The first house Meredith built was friendship. As a babe in arms she understood the basics of friendship. She spotted kindred spirits with a joyful "baby!" and a welcome wave. But her skills needed a little honing. Young Meredith's favorite place was the church nursery. There she had oodles of babies to play with. Her peers were a few months younger and not yet skilled in the fine art of walking. That was okay. Meredith played with them anyway. She walked up to each baby and gently tipped them over, one by one. The teachers rushed to the children's rescue, but just as they'd pick up one baby, Meredith would tip over another. Meredith wasn't trying to hurt her friends; they were just so perfectly posed with their crossed legs that they fell over smoothly. She saw them as big toys. Finally one teacher picked up Meredith.

To Spur Spirituality

True spirituality is a result of minute-by-minute personal choices. As our children choose to honor God, He equips them. We can offer ideas, promptings, examples, and structure to make our children's spiritual choices more likely:

Do you say what I say? Encourage your children to speak the words Jesus would speak, no matter who they're with or where they are. Suggest they ask: "Would I be pleased for Jesus to hear me say this?" "Would I want Him hearing me say it this way?" When a friend tells good news, for example, Jesus would likely say, "Tell me about it!" rather than, "So?"

Do you see what I see? Encourage your children to see things the way God sees them. A rainstorm can provide gorgeous dancing raindrops. A simple-looking person can be simply beautiful to be around. A free afternoon can be a chance to imagine rather than a sentence to boredom. Prompt your children to see and enjoy these treasures.

Light the pilot light: To discover what *Jesus would say* and *how He sees things*, encourage a daily quiet time with God—a devotional time or Bible reading time. Explain that this isn't the only time we spend with God, but it's the pilot light that gets the fire of devotion burning for the whole day. The best way to encourage personal Bible reading is to invite your children to join you with their Bibles in the same room while you read your Bible. Also, compliment your children when they read the Scriptures on their own, and invite them to share tidbits of what they discover.

Devotion as you go: Let day-by-day teaching supplement sit-down devotions. Teach as you go. "You've been wanting to talk more kindly. How has God been helping with that?" Invite your children to ask you similar questions. Let this kind of conversation communicate that God is a part of everyday life, not just Sundays or quiet times (Deuteronomy 6:6–7).

To Spur Spirituality (CONTINUED)

Make it a habit: Avoid "If you really loved Jesus, you'd find _____ easy." Expressing devotion to Jesus Christ isn't easy; that's why it's called "devotion." We must *commit* to quiet times, kindness, patience, and other Christian disciplines and then *keep at them*. Knowing it's going to be hard makes it easier for your child to stick with it and succeed. You can help your child along by suggesting the six-week test: do devotions, or speak kindly, or work on whatever Christian discipline, for six weeks. Research shows this helps us establish a *habit*.

Applaud small obediences: Working out arguments peacefully and welcoming a new friend to your school lunch table are as powerful as going to Africa as a missionary. It's being faithful with small things that most often ushers us into God's happiness (Matthew 25:23). Notice when your children do well, praise generously, and communicate that expressing Christianity brings happiness.

Play it again: Play Christian music exclusively from the time your children are babies. Christian music isn't soft versus loud, country versus rock. It's any musical style that tells the truth and encourages godly living. We remember and repeat in our minds any music we hear, from commercials to concerts. So choose songs by their lyrics. An easy-listening country song can encourage betrayal or lying, whereas a hard rock song can prompt God-centered loyalty to friends and family. Let the lyrics of the song and the lifestyle of the artist determine what music you'll buy and play.

Memorize Scripture: Find fun and natural ways to memorize Scripture. Set it to music. Rap it with a rhythm. Say it to a commercial jingle. Say how you'll live it. Challenge each other to memorize a verse a week. Take turns picking the passage. Your children will likely outdo you in this!

Meredith's mother was horrified upon hearing this. Meredith's father was delighted. "Nobody's going to push our little girl around. She can stand up for herself!" But both took seriously their responsibility of guiding Meredith to an *Oh!* experience.

"Meredith, when you knock over the babies, you hurt them. Jesus wants us to be kind to our friends," they explained. At eighteen months, Meredith wasn't quite able to grasp this cognitively. But she did understand "no" and she did understand "ouch." So her parents volunteered in the nursery a couple times to help Meredith understand how to love her friends with *outward faithfulness*. Each time she started to tip a baby, they moved her back and firmly said "No, Meredith! That will hurt Jesse. He'd say, 'Ouch!' Sit down next to him and roll the ball instead."

Sometimes Meredith would roll the ball to her friend. Other times she'd feel so sad at being corrected that she'd go off and sit by herself with big tears in her eyes. But after several corrections, Meredith would toddle toward her friends, quietly saying to herself, "No, Mer'dith. No hurt. Roll ball." Then she'd sit down rather than tip. In the absence of Meredith's parents, the nursery teachers reinforced these people lessons, just as they taught Meredith to blow bubbles, to sniff flowers, and to wave out the window at people coming to church. Friendship is a skill to be learned.

Grade-school-aged Meredith still enjoyed activity, but hated the telephone. She needed a little *tenacity* to overcome her dislike of this kind of communication. When a friend called she'd answer with single words and close the conversation with a single-syllable "bye." She practiced her *speaking skills* with her grandmother as guinea pig. Her mother also insisted that she asked at least one question each time a friend called. They listed together fifty questions she could ask: "How do you think you did on the math test today?" "I liked the way you play soccer—how long have you been playing?" and more. Each time she asked more than one question, her mother gave her a quarter. Bit by bit, Meredith gained confidence on the telephone. It never became her favorite mode of communication, but she used it lovingly.

Meredith used her *Oh!* experiences to express *outward faithfulness* to her baby peers, to her childhood phone mates, to her high school soul mates. She learned to laugh at her own mistakes and successes with a delight that was contagious, and with an I-care-about-you-attitude that made peers feel loved to their toes. Her *tenacity* enabled her to talk on the phone in ways that communicated care rather than rotely answered questions. It equipped her to stick with her commitment to cut cruel words from her vocabulary. Her *speaking skills* enabled her to hear people's hearts and treasure their secrets.

Put the Right People on the Job

Young Tyrone also built houses of friendship. As he grew his parents noticed and highlighted his amazing gift of people-loving. He naturally saw the good in people and he liked what he saw. His parents guided him to harness and refine his extraordinary speaking skills to invite others to share themselves. As they hoped, he was just as able to get others to talk as he was able to talk himself. Just as he found the details in their lives interesting, he was able to get them to believe in themselves. He discovered (Oh!) the lovely gift of mutual edification: each working for the other's joy, family and friends caring equally for each other.

> Will they cherish each other with consistent acts of kindness and interest? Or will they expect the fairy tale to just happen and blame each other when it doesn't?

"Tyrone, ask Alex about his camping trip," his parents would prompt. "Be sure to tell him what you think is fascinating about what he says."

At first Tyrone would ask a question and then launch back into his own narratives. But person by person, he learned to focus on others. By the time he was in middle school, he still told plenty of stories, but he listened more than he spoke. He paid such close attention to people that they felt deeply important. Friends loved telling Tyrone their thoughts and ideas. He affirmed each comment, and gently prodded the speaker to think further about inconsistencies or untruths. He applauded on-target conclusions. Tyrone's parents helped him turn his storytelling tenacity into people-interest.

Prepare for Something Bigger

Meredith's parents and Tyrone's parents have prayed for their children's spouses from the time they were tiny babies. They prayed that the parents of those spouses-to-be would raise them toward Christlikeness and show them how to love in uncomplicated and straightforward ways. Then, recognizing that someone might be praying for their children, they worked to raise their own children toward Christlikeness.

Seldom was the teaching easy. Occasionally it was particularly heart wrenching. But still they continued. As a fifth grader Tyrone went through a painful time of self-doubt. He began to refrain from his finest gift—telling about real people. He feared people would think his stories were silly. His parents suffered almost as deeply as Tyrone during this time, but they guided him to *Oh!* experiences that deepened his confidence. First they assured him that feeling lonely and self-conscious didn't mean he was unaccepted, boring, or ugly. These feelings meant he was eleven, twelve, or thirteen years old. All middle schoolers felt at least occasional sadness, self-doubt, and confusion. Armed with understanding, Tyrone was better able to battle the hounding hormones that tormented him, better able to believe his worth. His parents refused to laugh at his fears or questions. Instead, they answered them. They assured Tyrone those feelings made good sense and showed him what to do about them.

"If you feel a little ugly, avoid mirrors," they advised. "And when you do look, find at least one good-looking quality about yourself. Check out your radiant eyes or your easy smile. God made you good—see His handiwork."

"When you feel left out of a group, look around for someone else who might be feeling the same way," they suggested on other days. "Of all the people in the room, 99.9% are wondering if anyone wants to talk to them. Make the first move to make the whole group more loving."

Because Tyrone's parents cherished him and equipped him, he was able to build a healthy relationship with Meredith, not a clingy one. Meredith's parents gave her similar skills. During her self-doubting years, her dad made the big difference. The two went out to eat weekly and he gave her his undivided attention as she told him the details of her daily experiences. This *Oh!* experience helped her recognize guys—and parents—as people who care, people to talk to and listen to. Meredith's security in her father/daughter relationship gave her the peace and talking skills she needed to relate to guys as friends rather than potential dates. While Meredith's girlfriends went *gaa-gaa* over guys, she calmly grew friendships with them. Certainly there were deep feelings and emotional times. But underlying all was a river of security that gave her a foundation for true closeness.

Love doesn't just happen. It's built through a lifetime of prac-tice—practical application of principles to real circumstances. Mer-edith was anxious for Tyrone to ask her out but tempered her ea-gerness with an understanding that the best relationships grow slowly, and the best romances are based in solid friendship. She then used this *Oh!* discovery to relax and enjoy Tyrone's outward faith-fulness expressed so naturally in his friendship to her and to every other person he encountered. Tyrone treated every person as if he or she were the only person in the world. Interestingly, this seldom made Meredith jealous. Instead it made her proud to be friends with such a caring person. It made her want to show the same outward faithfulness to her friends and family. She found herself listening more, and commenting with interest on whatever people told her.

Keep Your Work Site Clean

Tyrone and Meredith married recently. Will they live happily ever after? That's up to them. Happy marriages aren't made in fairy tales; they're made in real houses where real people choose to act in caring ways. Tyrone's and Meredith's happiness as friends, spouses, and par-ents depends on their choices. Will they approach life as an adven-ture with God, constantly finding resourceful ways to serve Him in day-to-day existence? Or will they whine about the inconveniences and troubles that come their way? Will they actively cherish each other with consistent acts of interest and kindness? Or will they expect the fairy tale to just happen and blame each other when it doesn't? Will they enjoy the good in each other? Or will they compete with and criticize each other? Will they choose to solve problems with unity or bickering? Will they disagree with grace or judgment?

It's their choice.

Tyrone and Meredith will have opportunity after opportunity to choose the loving way over the divisive one. One of their first opportunities came as newlyweds. Tyrone, trying to be thoughtful, complimented Meredith on the baked potatoes she served for supper. Meredith was surprised. Hers was only half cooked. She had been chiding herself for not timing them right. *He must like them that way*, she reasoned.

So she regularly took his potato out thirty minutes before hers. She set it on top of the toaster oven where it stayed warm without cooking the rest of the way. Six months later Tyrone finally said, "Honey, I've tried to be nice. But could you please cook these baked potatoes a little longer?"

Meredith, mouth full of potato, burst into laughter. Tears were rolling down her face when she finally caught her breath enough to explain. "I'm so sorry! I thought you liked them that way! I've been taking yours out thirty minutes early!"

A confused Tyrone now got tickled and gave her a big hug.

They had an *Oh!* discovery: kindness is important but it must be honest. This discovery never would have happened without sensitive speaking and caring humor. Meredith and Tyrone laughed *with* each other rather than *at* each other. And Meredith shared half of her perfectly done potato with Tyrone.

On to their next adventure.

Thanks to parents and grandparents who cared enough to equip them with love-building tools, Tyrone and Meredith can climb the mountain of life together. They can let their enjoyment of each other spill over into their parenting, their friendships, their church membership, their jobs, their neighboring. All they have to do is choose to take the steps.

Joy Tip

Love doesn't just happen. It requires choosing to bring honest closeness. See each encounter with your children not as a stage, but as an opportunity to teach them love skills, the tools that will enhance their friendships, their marriage, and their own parenting.

4

BUT HE DOESN'T WANT TO

No discipline seems pleasant at the time, but painful. Later on, however, it produces a harvest of righteousness and peace for those who have been trained by it.

—Hebrews 12:11

You know the ones. She takes a second turn when everyone else is waiting for a first. He pushes his way to the front of the line. She talks the whole time others are talking. He plays with ice cream rather than eating it. She takes the biggest donut. He laughs at everyone else's expense. She calls every game babyish or stupid. He quits when he doesn't win. She gossips profusely, but cries when someone says anything ugly about her. He acts like an angel while you're watching, but does just the opposite behind your back. You know the one. You've lost count of the teachers who have retired when this child is promoted into their Sunday school class.

With what word do you describe this child? Brat? Obnoxious? Spoiled? Selfish? Rude? Bully? Mean? Jerk? Whatever word you use, this child is no fun to be around. In fact, you dread his presence. Why? He lacks a crucial tool for happiness: self-discipline. He does only what he wants, only when he feels like doing it. He doesn't care a whit about how his actions impact anyone else. He sees little relationship between what he does and how God might want him to act. He assumes that his every problem is someone else's fault.

This child is a crystal clear illustration that enjoyment only grows when discipline has taken root. It's discipline that makes it possible for you—and other people in and outside your family—to enjoy your children. And for your children to enjoy other people!

Rita and Zach found their family mulling this point one day after church:

"Sam makes me so mad!" Keisha said. "This morning when the teacher offered the leftover donuts to me for our lunch, Sam jumped in and said, 'Sure, I'll take them!' Then he grabbed them. I finally talked him into giving me half. But the teacher hadn't offered him any at all. He'd already eaten half a dozen during class. Now there aren't even enough for each of us to have one."

"He always does stuff like that," added Jerome. "He hogs class time too. It's as though he thinks his stories are the only ones worth telling."

"Once he starts nobody else gets a word in," said Keisha. "If we do say anything, Sam has to add some editorial comment. He drives me crazy."

"Yeah, and he asks for stuff," said Jerome. "When I gave Andy a birthday gift, Sam said, 'My birthday is in two weeks. What are you going to bring me?' He didn't even say 'Happy Birthday' to Andy. That makes me never want to give him anything!"

Rita and Zach listened while their children unloaded.

"How would you like it if someone felt that way about you?" Zach eventually asked.

"I'd hate it," Keisha responded. "That would be terrible."

"But I wouldn't treat people the way he does," offered Jerome. "It's his fault people think this way about him."

"It is hard to enjoy someone who focuses on themselves," agreed Rita.

"That's why we were strict on you two yesterday when you were arguing over computer time. Nobody likes somebody who doesn't take turns," Zach explained.

"Or who hogs donuts, or talking time, or attention," added Keisha.

"Exactly," said Rita.

"I was pretty mad at you yesterday for making me get off the computer," said Jerome. "You seemed like the meanest parents in the world."

"We felt that way too," said Zach. "It's not easy to make you be good. That's probably why Sam's parents don't do it. It's much easier to let him talk, to let him take. We parents can excuse stuff like that with, 'Well it's just this once' or 'He's young.' "

"But then he drives everybody crazy," said Jerome.

"Yes, he does," said Zach. "That's what we try to keep in mind when you're mad at us for insisting that you be kind."

"I hate being the heavy," added Rita. "You look so sad and you say stuff like, 'But I was just getting to the good part in the game! Please don't make me stop now!' "

"It would be much easier to let you keep playing. In fact, I'd like to let you," said Zach. "But then Keisha would have to wait and wait."

"Yeah, like Sam makes us do whenever we play any kind of game where we have to take turns," said Keisha with renewed frustration. "I hate playing with him."

"What you do and say determines whether people want to be around you or not," agreed Rita. "Jesus knows what He's talking about when He says, 'Love your neighbor as yourself' in Matthew 22:39."

"Sam loves himself as himself," added Jerome one last time.

"Often he does. But if we aren't careful, we'll be setting ourselves higher than him," prompted Zach. "And when we're watching someone else, we don't notice our own faults."

"I get it," responded Keisha. "You want us to make ourselves be good, not try to get others to be good."

"It certainly is more effective," said Rita.

"And you want us to be as caring as we want Sam to be," added Jerome.

"That's right," said Zach. "When you choose to care on your own, then Mom and I won't need to enforce it. It's called self-discipline."

"It sounds more like just being nice," said Keisha.

"That's definitely part of it," added Rita. "It's choosing to treat people the same way Jesus Christ would. Sometimes that means being nice. Sometimes it means being firm. All the time it means doing right, no matter how tough."

Discipline is harder than it sounds, and our children won't automatically understand why we do what we do. I've yet to meet a child who thanks his parents for disciplining him at the time the discipline takes place. But as Zach and Rita discovered, children can grasp the hows and whys of discipline. They can understand that

- Discipline isn't control or punishment.
- Discipline is guidance, showing our children how to live delightfully, honestly, and fairly with other people.
- Discipline is pointing out the loving path, the path that brings happiness to both us and those around us.
- Discipline is structure. Just as the skeleton provides a frame for the body, structure provides opportunities to choose to love God and people.
- Discipline is leading with such clear communication and reliable consistency that our children eventually choose the right path on their own.

Tackle the Toughness of the Task

If Rita and Zach's children understand the basics of discipline—and if Rita and Zach mean well when they discipline—why do their kids have trouble accepting it? Because whether you're a child or an adult, it's hard to change. It's not easy to reach outside yourself to love someone else. Keisha and Jerome would rather go ahead and play that computer game, whether right or wrong. So they push to be able to do that. Like almost every kid alive, they know how to give that hurt puppy look. Or how to declare that if their parents really cared, they wouldn't be so mean.

Kids also have trouble accepting discipline because they sense when a parent's resolve is wavering. When Rita and Zach struggle with being the heavy, Keisha and Jerome know it. If their parents are uncertain, maybe it really is okay to keep doing what they're doing rather than take turns or speak kindly. So Keisha and Jerome find another way to get what they're after. They'll sneak that extra turn on the computer or say something mean to their brother when Dad's not looking. They'll avoid picking up their room if there's any way they can.

> Rather than seeing discipline as an us-against-our-kids battle, recognize it as a shared human predicament.

This isn't evil. It's selfish. It's convenient. It's human nature.

All of us would rather focus on ourselves than cooperate with someone else. This persistent bent is exactly why we must follow our words with actions. We must be vigilant and consistent to guide our children down the good and fair path. Rather than see discipline as an us-against-our-kids battle, it's our task to recognize it as a shared human predicament (Romans 7:14–8:4). Weren't you just as stubborn, perhaps more so, as a child? And don't those same characteristics continue today if you don't keep them in check? Only through the grace of God and the effort of parents or other adults who cared about you did you change from selfish to self-disciplined.

Do your children the same favor. Teach them the freedom of discipline. Give them the security of structure. Grant them the foundation of follow-through. Discipline is hard. Our kids won't like it. But it's a critical skill for life enjoyment, for life success.

Keep the Goal in Mind

If discipline is so hard and people are so hesitant to change for the better, why not just give in and live according to our human nature? Because it's lonely. Sam can't grow a real friendship because he won't reach beyond his own needs to care about someone else. If we don't move past our human tendency to take what we want when we want it, we grow to be adults who go to bed when there's tough work to be done and then miraculously recover when the party begins. Or we become the Hitlers who blame and attack everyone but themselves for the problems they have. It looks like power, but it's really isolation. We miss the joy of mutual effort, of giving to others, of sacrificing so someone else can be happy. And we stay very, very lonely.

We don't have to settle for this agony. We and our children can rise above our selfish nature to show care. We can cooperate rather than assume everyone has to do things our way.

We can do right rather than lie and betray to get what we want. We can seek to serve, rather than assume others are here to make us happy. Jesus thought of it first. We know it as the Golden Rule: "Do to others as you would have them do to you" (Luke 6:31).

It won't be easy, but we and our children can do it. How? Through God's power. The Bible describes the process this way: "For what the law was powerless to do . . . God did by sending his own

"WHEN I GROW UP, I'M GOING TO BE NICE TO MY KIDS"

Do you give in to your child's pleading eyes and sad words? Learn to respond rather than react. As you explain your actions, your children can know *why* you do *what* you do. It's a tactic that not only helps the present but also makes it easier for your children to discipline themselves later.

If your child says...	Respond with...
"You're so mean!"	"I don't intend to be mean. I just want you to be a loving person."
"But we don't want to go to sleep."	"It is hard to stop the fun. But if you don't rest tonight you'll be too tired to have fun tomorrow. If you don't quiet down you'll need to take a nap tomorrow."
"You made me quit in the middle of a game."	"No, you didn't finish your chore before you started the game. You made it necessary to quit in order to complete the chore."
"Jerome, you're a brat. I wish you weren't my brother."	"You can be frustrated with your brother but you can't talk to him like that. Speak to him the way you want him to talk to you."
"Why do I have to pick up my room?"	"So you can find things when you're looking for them."
"But I don't feel like it."	"Nobody feels like it. But it has to be done. So get it over with."

"WHEN I GROW UP, I'M GOING TO BE NICE TO MY KIDS" (CONTINUED)

If your child says...	Respond with...
"My kids won't have to eat broccoli."	"But you do. You need the nutrients. After you eat it you can have dessert. Until you eat it you'll have nothing else."
"It's not fair that I have to do the dishes."	"It's very fair. We all share chores so we can all share the free time."
"Please let me have the last cookie! I called it first."	"Yes, you called it, but both of you want it. Cut it in half, and Keisha will choose. That keeps it even."
"I want to ride the go-carts again."	"But you spent all your money on the other rides."
"Please give me some more money."	"Before we came we agreed to spend $10 apiece. We warned you, but you spent all yours early. Maybe next time you'll find it easier to save."
"You don't love me."	"Because I love you I insist that you do right."
"Daddy, Mama doesn't love me."	"You can't play us against each other. I know Mama loves you, and you know Mama loves you. To say otherwise is a lie. You must do what she says."

Don't expect your children to applaud your discipline. But do expect them to do good because of it. Explain, then carry out the discipline. Tell the reasons for your discipline, not to replace action, but to reinforce it.

Son in the likeness of sinful man" (Romans 8:3). Rules, even insight into our bad behaviors, won't change us. Only God himself can make us good. As we and our children choose to become Christians and daily call on His Spirit, both parental discipline and self-discipline become effective.

If you and your children haven't already become Christians, I invite you to do so now. Admit your sin to God. Sin is the tendency in all of us to do wrong. Then pray and ask Jesus Christ to cleanse and forgive you. God will immediately give you a fresh start. He will live in you through His Holy Spirit, and He will guide you to recognize and choose good. He will give you the power to carry out your good choices.

Go for the Gold

Even with all these good results waiting to happen and all these destructive consequences at stake, it's hard to always be in the position of having to make our children mind. We'd much rather take the easy-for-the-moment action:

- "It won't hurt to let her do that just this once. Besides—today is her birthday."
- "If that's the worst he ever does, we'll be fine."
- "Boys will be boys."

Like an Olympic medalist, we've got to do the hard-for-now thing to bring the joy-for-later things. It's a process of learning to "live a life worthy of the calling you have received" (Ephesians 4:1). We must guide our children to be Christlike in their attitudes and actions. When we've told our teen he must finish the lawn before going out that evening and he dawdles the afternoon away, we must follow through by keeping him home to finish, even if his friends are knocking at the door. We've got to insist that the birthday girl include her brother so she realizes that the big day is meant to give joy to everyone, not to make her the center of attention.

Discipline is a daily workout. But the gold at the end is worth it. If we look closely, we see markers of success almost immediately. Discipline brings kind words when cruel ones were threatened. Discipline gives everyone equal attention, turns, rest, and work. Discipline promotes enjoyment and togetherness—a family that likes each other. Discipline prevents fear. It's scary to be able to manipulate people, especially people who are bigger than you. That's one reason unruly children are so angry. Watch their faces. They're frightened and out of control. They may call this "nobody tells me what to do" or "I don't have to obey any rules." But their hearts feel that "no one cares enough to help me behave."

Cherish your child's heart and mind with discipline. Give her the security of knowing there are limits she can count on. Give him the confidence of knowing that if he doesn't know how to handle a situation, you'll be there to help.

Determine the Best Strategy

"I don't like our church anymore, Mom!" protested Jerome. "I don't belong there. Can't I just stay home?"

"But you've been attending since you were a baby, Jerome. You have tons of friends there. What makes you say you don't belong?" Rita responded through an anguished heart. What could be wrong? Nobody belonged in their church more than Jerome. Why this sudden change?

> Enjoyment and discipline aren't opposites—good discipline makes it possible for you and others to enjoy your children.

"Nobody talks to me," explained Jerome. "Ever since I came into the youth group, everybody's got their own little groups, and I'm not in any of them."

"Oh, that does sound rough," responded Rita, wanting to support her son but unsure of what it all meant. Pictures of her own church experience came back to her. She too had grown up in church. She too wanted to quit in the eighth grade. Do I make him go or not? If her parents hadn't made her go, she definitely would have quit church. She decided to ask for more information.

"How long have you been feeling this way, Jerome?" she asked, remembering several recent Sundays when he'd dragged his feet about getting ready for church. Maybe the change hadn't been that sudden after all.

"Forever," said Jerome miserably. "You don't know how bad it is, Mom."

The mother-bear emotion rose up in Rita. She was primed to do anything to protect her cub. But because a swipe of her paw couldn't slice away this problem, she told the mother-bear to calm down and invited God's guiding hand to take its place.

"I think I understand," she said.

"Josh has quit coming," said Jerome. "Can't I just stay home from youth Sunday school for a month or two? Maybe things will be better by then."

"I don't think that's the best solution," said Rita. "It's not you, and it's not the group. Staying away could solve those problems, but it won't solve this one. We need some friendship-building instead. We need shared experiences—that's how friendships grow. If you stay away you'll feel more and more isolated."

"But I already feel isolated," Jerome repeated.

"I know the feeling," Rita commiserated. "But I think the problem isn't that you don't belong, but that you feel all new—that what you used to like you don't like so much anymore, or that the friends you used to have maybe aren't your friends now. Most of the other seventh, eighth, and ninth graders at our church probably feel left out too."

"How can you know that?" asked Jerome, incredulous.

"Because all young teenagers feel like whole new people, because most youth struggle to belong, and because I felt that way myself," said Rita.

"You? But you've been in church forever," said Jerome, unable to believe his outgoing mother had ever had trouble feeling at home.

"Yes, me," Rita confirmed. "I'll never forget how awful going to church felt when I was thirteen. If my parents hadn't made me keep going, I would have certainly dropped out. I didn't know it then, but I realize now that there's no way to feel instantly at home. When I meet a new group of co-workers, I seldom feel at home. It's only after we've attacked a project together for a while that I feel a part of things."

"But I feel so uncomfortable there!" insisted Jerome. "Especially without Josh."

"Believe me, I remember," said Rita. "And you'll miss Josh a lot. But the way to fit in is to keep going. Each week you share more experiences and develop a deeper relationship with the others in your Bible study group. Because you do things together, like study the Bible and talk in the hall before and after class, you'll begin to feel a part of each other. You'll grow fellowship."

"I've been doing all that, and I still hate church," said Jerome. "Can't I just stay out a couple months?"

"No, you've got to keep going. Once you quit, you'll find it harder and harder to go back," said Rita. "The difference this time is you'll know what's going on, and you can do something about it. Rather than wait for people to talk to you, start conversations. Find somebody else who's standing alone."

"But there isn't anybody," insisted Jerome.

"Then pick twosomes, or trios," said Rita, ninety-nine percent sure she was right. "It will be hard but you can do it. And please let me know how it goes."

"Ohh-kayy," said Jerome reluctantly.

Rita gave Jerome guidance, the form of discipline that helps kids know what to do. Discipline isn't just correcting misbehavior and rewarding good behavior. It's firmly but kindly guiding our children down paths that lead to success. Discipline makes sure our kids follow through with the hard but healthy choices until they're old enough to do it on their own.

Rita's decision about how to guide Jerome was prompted by her own teenage suffering and reinforced by the sad experience of another family in their church. That couple had let their son stay home from Sunday morning Bible study when he began resisting. They said he must come to worship, but could skip Sunday school for a while. When time came for him to return to Sunday school, he felt like such a stranger that he hated it even more than before. He returned to worship attendance only. Because he didn't come to Sunday school, he sometimes missed his chance to flock into church with all the other youth. He didn't want to look stupid and walk to where the teens sat together, so he just sat alone in the back. Gradually, he had fewer and fewer contacts with the other kids from church. When he got his driver's license he came separately from his parents and sometimes arrived late. Once he was so late he decided he'd better not interrupt worship. He just stayed in his car. Eventually he quit participating in worship altogether. His parents still pray he'll come back and that he'll feel welcome. But his ties are cut so completely that he feels no pull to return.

Jerome and this young man needed prompting to establish the ties that bind, the ties that make us feel a part of the body of Jesus Christ. The one factor that gives us church membership is our salvation; but the factor that makes us feel at home with the membership is time together. Jerome won't feel at home *instantly*, but he will feel at home *eventually* as he week-by-week shares Bible study and time talking with his peers.

Give 110 Percent

Rita was worn out after helping Jerome find an answer, and the work wasn't over with that one conversation. Each Saturday evening brought new concerns: Would Jerome enjoy a conversation with anyone? Would a friendship bridge be built? Each Sunday morning brought fresh questions. Would Bible study be a bore—or challenging enough to be interesting? Would the teachers appreciate Jerome's contributions and the contributions of others? Would they just stand up and lecture, or would they use Bible study methods that encouraged interaction with the Bible and with each other? Rita tried to ready Jerome for all this, calming her spirit so she would be helpful rather than agitated.

It was tough to be the adult, the one to motivate Jerome to take the hard-for-now, happier-for-later path. But she did it for Jerome's sake. She chose to draw on other families' experiences, and her slow but sure success with making it through feelings of alienation at church. She opened herself to find out what she didn't yet know: how to make the Sunday school hour the place where belonging can take place. She talked to youth workers to find out what she could do to help. She committed herself to weave God's truth that real fellowship is best with real believers on a regular basis around every feeling and concern (2 Corinthians 6:14; Hebrews 10:25). All this took enormous energy. But Rita found her fatigue worth it, a sweet tired, filled with hope for victory.

At first glance it looked like Sam, the donut-grabber, was the one who was given freedom. But with that free rein, he lost good friends, lost the ability to relate with mutual respect, lost the intimacy that would ease his loneliness. Jerome on the other hand stayed in a tough new situation. Which is real freedom? Which is real restriction? Jerome's statement four months later answers the question: "I wish I could go to church all day every day, and school just on Sunday mornings and Wednesday nights. I love the people in our youth group."

A Dozen Ways to Discipline

As Jerome's mother discovered, discipline is so much more than spanking and grounding. It's providing the structure that enables our children to choose the loving and good path. Here are a dozen ideas:

A Way With Words: When your children speak cruelly to each other, provide—and insist they use—substitute words that say the same thing without the hurt. "Please knock and wait for me to answer" is better than, "You have absolutely no respect for anyone's privacy!" "What you're doing is really irritating me" is better than, "You are impossible to live with!" Even better, prompt your children to translate their caustic words and attitudes to their own kind ones. Prompt them with "Is there a better way you can say that?"

Let the Punishment Fit the Crime: If your child got a bad grade, extra study time is a better punishment than grounding. If bedtime is 8:30 and your child consistently dawdles until 9:00, make Friday bedtime 8:00 or earlier. If your child breaks a sibling's toy, have her replace it with her own money, earning money she doesn't yet have.

Let the Reward Fit the Responsible Behavior: Conversely, if your child earns a good grade, give thirty minutes off from afternoon studying. If your child consistently goes to bed on time, let him stay up later on Friday nights. If your child treats a sibling's possession with care, get her one of her own.

Return the Candy: Guide your child to follow a wrong deed with a corrective one. He returns the candy taken from the checkout counter and apologizes to the cashier. As your child experiences the results of wrong behaviors, he'll find it easier to think through consequences. Important: Lessons will be different with the age of the child. Very small children don't realize it's wrong to take the candy home from the store without paying for it. They learn that the candy belongs to someone else. Older children may try to get away with shoplifting. Returning the candy reinforces that crime doesn't pay.

Map a Strategy Together: Invite your children to decide a plan, rewards, and punishments to solve the problem. If he doesn't bring his clothes to the hamper and then complains because his clothes aren't washed, ask: How can we make sure your clothes get to the laundry hamper in time? Avoid accusation and promote a team spirit.

Instant Replay: When your children come home in agony over failing a test or arguing with a friend, guide them to discover what to do by replaying the situation. Ask, "What happened, step by step?" "What would you change if you could go through the experience again?" "What do you think God would want you to do if you could play the whole thing over?" "What does God want you to do since you *can't* play it over?" Instant replay helps children think about how to manage tough situations before they're in the middle of them again. A verbal child can talk with you about what to do. A less verbal child can make a comic strip or write a story. A very young child can draw what happened and how he wants it to happen next time.

Whistle While You Work: Getting work done is part of a disciplined life. Agree with your child that few people enjoy vacuuming, mowing the lawn, or taking the car to the repair shop. But they have to be done—so challenge your child to do it better than before, to whistle, to solve a problem while they work. Invite your child to devise his own make-the-mundane-marvelous method.

Reward the Truth: As a child I knew that if I told the truth about a wrong I'd done, I'd get consequences, but the punishment would be less severe. If I tried to hide the truth, the punishment was fourfold greater when the truth was discovered (as it always was). Be stiff on lying. Telling the truth is the basis for trust.

Do What You Say You Will Do: Give your children the security of knowing you mean what you say. If you say he must finish homework before watching television, don't let him watch even if it's the ending to a two-part episode of his favorite show. It will hurt you, but it will hurt him more to miss learning how to budget his time.

Success Markers: When your child brings home schoolwork, discuss together what needs to get done and how much time will be needed to do it. Let him know when there's two hours, one hour, and then thirty minutes to go so he can end on time.

Celebrate Sucess: When your child completes homework early or does an especially kind action, offer an especially fun free-time activity such as extra computer time or a walk with you. Generously praise his good use of time and excellent choice.

Be the Heavy: Children adore sleepovers. But the all-consuming fatigue from staying up all night makes it impossible to enjoy the next day. If you're consistent with a predetermined time for lights out, they can go ahead and sleep without looking like babies. Once you've announced bedtime, sit in the next room until you're certain all are asleep.

Smooth Out Your Moves

Kindness and goodness are anything but wimpy. They require a muscular commitment to stand for right no matter what or who opposes it. So along with Zach and Rita, build these muscles in your children by exercising discipline. Working out isn't much fun; but the power that results is worth the work. Swallow your fears and stir up your compassion. God knows your needs, and He will equip you. His Word reminds us that "No discipline seems pleasant at the time, but painful. Later on, however, it produces a harvest of righteousness and peace for those who have been trained by it" (Hebrews 12:11). Like a good athlete who's running for the distance, evaluate your moves. Find out just what to improve to bring a harvest of righteousness and peace to your children.

Expand Your Capacity: Do you need to expand your discipline methods? As we have said, discipline is much more than spanking and grounding. It's acting in ways that end the bad and increase the good. Discipline gets most of its bad press because of its connection with spanking, and a faulty view that identifies it as punishment. But punishment is only a tiny part of discipline, and spanking is only one kind of punishment. Spanking works only for certain cases and certain ages. Discover strategies that work more widely. Spanking worked well for young Jerome when he'd done a deliberate wrong and tried to get away with it. But when his temper was out of control, spanking only made things worse; it became a stand-off Jerome was determined to win. Much more effective was, "Go to your room and get it together. When you're ready to be kind, come out, and we'll talk."

How do you tell if your method is the right one? Notice the results. Spanking quieted Jerome for a few seconds, and then he exploded with even greater intensity. Thinking in his room quieted his temper so he could talk things out cooperatively. Doing nothing kept tension high in the family. Based on these results, separation was the best discipline method for dispelling Jerome's rage. Even better, it still works now that he's a teenager.

Use Opposing Muscle Groups: It takes opposing muscles working together to move your arms and legs. Discipline discovers the opposing muscle groups of child-rearing. What's called for at the moment? Do you need restricting—or prompting—to move your children in the right direction? In addition to the child who bullies his way through life, there are children who hold back and miss much good. Keisha is so gentle she lets everyone go first and then grieves because all the good stuff is gone by the time she redeems her carnival tickets. Keisha needs prompting to go ahead and act. This assertiveness isn't pushiness or meanness, but dedication to right. It's the same fervent commitment that made Jesus turn the tables in the temple. Good requires action. For Keisha to be fair in line, to stand up for a friend, to right a wrong, to do a good, she must not hold back. Her parents discipline her with steady nudges and practice in making the first move.

Give Permission to Speak Freely: Athletes often know the areas that need work before the coach does. Invite your children to approach you similarly. Even a toddler can voice what he did wrong. A preschooler can suggest good actions to do instead of the bad one. School-age children can write prayer letters to God about what they did wrong or failed to do right, and add how to do right the next time. High-schoolers can set some of their own restrictions and rewards. Because the ultimate goal of discipline is *self*-discipline, your children's involvement makes it possible for them to choose right on their own.

Discipline gets a bad name when it's equated with do-what-mom-and-dad-say-without-question. We parents do have more experience, but we aren't perfect. And some parents are downright unfair. To avoid this, include your child's input in your discipline: "What's wrong about this action or attitude?" "Why might I be upset about it?" "What would stop it?" "What good action could replace it?" "How could I make it easier for you to choose what's right?"

Hearing your children isn't the same as letting them have free rein; it's helping your child pinpoint what they need to do and why. Hearing your children keeps up your end of the parent/child relationship. It heeds the biblical command, "Do not exasperate your children; instead, bring them up in the training and instruction of the Lord" (Ephesians 6:4).

Follow Through: It's easy to neglect exercise. But it shows in your performance. Discipline is similar. At first only you and your children know that you haven't followed through. But it doesn't take long for friends, teachers, and even strangers to notice that your child lacks the ability to get along with others.

Keisha knows exactly the times she must heed her parents' words. When they're busily working in the yard and send her in to bed, she knows she can always stay up at least thirty minutes later because her folks lose track of time and don't come in to turn out her lights. Keisha needs actions to follow the instructions.

Zach knows he's weak on follow-through. "I really mean for Keisha to get to bed on time. But I get distracted with my garden. Lately I've noticed she delays not only bedtime but other things until I tell her a second time. We're establishing a dangerous pattern, one that says, 'I don't really have to do this if nobody's watching.' How will she ever do right on her own? So last week I started to set a timer for *myself*, just like we do with computer turns for the kids. Then when it goes off I go in to check her. Now that I'm checking her more consistently, she gets into bed on time. Because she's had enough sleep, she wakens more cheerfully in the morning. That makes all of us happier."

> In your garden of family happiness, the weeds of selfishness and cruelty will threaten to choke out joy. Persistently pull these weeds through godly discipline.

Study Under Good Coaches: The best athletes seek experienced and effective coaches. We parents weren't born knowing how to discipline. So learn from those who have parented before you. Check with your own parents and other parents who have raised caring children. What did they do that worked? What would they change if they could raise their kids again? What would they definitely repeat? How would they handle the challenge you presently face? Invite those you particularly trust to observe your parenting and make suggestions for improvement (on a day you feel secure!). Urge them to pray with you as you refine your skills. The friends in the faith who have walked this path before us are there to help. "Therefore, since we are surrounded by such a great cloud of witnesses, let us throw off everything that hinders and the sin that so easily entangles, and let us run with perseverance the race marked out for us. Let us fix our eyes on Jesus, the author and perfecter of our faith" (Hebrews 12:1–2).

Magnify the Good Moves

In your garden of family happiness, weeds of selfishness and cruelty threaten to choke out joy. Persistently pull these weeds through godly discipline. Then watch. As in a garden, the joy-giving habit becomes strong enough to choke out the weeds of selfishness.

In the process your child becomes the one who listens eagerly to the news of others before telling her stories. The one who helps everyone get an equal turn. The one who suggests that two lines form so all can get their food more quickly. The one who says thanks for the ice cream. The one who splits the cookies equally. The one who has genuine fun in every game he tries. The one who says "good try" when another makes a mistake and "good game" when another wins. The one you can trust to do right whether you're watching or not. The one who keeps secrets. The one who repeats only what is kind.

You know the ones. The ones you invite to your house with pleasure. The ones you're glad to have as your children's friends. The ones you hope join, or teach, your Sunday school class. The one you hope your son will date. The one you pray your daughter will marry.

Joy Tip

Guide your children to reach beyond themselves and treat others as they'd like to be treated. Insist on their choosing this good path until they are ready to choose that path for themselves.

5

HAPPINESS SOLD SEPARATELY

Prepare the way for the Lord, make straight paths for him.

—Luke 3:4

The day started like a storybook. In the predawn hours Meg and Ted woke to the subdued giggles of children whispering a bit too loudly in the next room. Dan and Sasha were putting final touches on a Christmas surprise they'd sneakily planned for weeks. Meg and Ted smiled sleepily, unable to hear exactly what their children were up to but knowing it would be good. Certain that their children would waken at 2:00 A.M. if permitted, Ted had told the children they could go to each other's rooms no earlier than 6:45 and that they'd start Christmas not a second before 7:00.

Precisely at 7:00 the door burst open, the light flipped on, and Meg and Ted beheld Dan and Sasha in costumes they couldn't identify. Each wore an unusual paper hat and a label that said "100 percent Sweet." Each carried a meter that said "Full." Each was splashed with ribbons and bows.

"We're sweet and thoughtful children!" they burst out, unable to wait for a guess. Ted and Meg then saw THOUGHTS on their full meters. "See? Our thought meters are full and we're sweet like a chocolate bar from our hats to our toes."

Ted and Meg laughed until they cried. Every year their children asked what Ted and Meg wanted for Christmas. Every year Ted and Meg chimed the same response: "All we want is for you to be sweet and thoughtful children." Dan and Sasha were delighted with themselves that they had finally given their parents just what they asked for.

Meg was bursting with happiness. The creativity and love of this gift filled her up and warmed her through and through. It struck her as the most meaningful present she had ever received. If Christmas had ended right there she'd have been delighted.

But the children, of course, wanted their gifts. So they unloaded their stockings on the sofa and then made their way to the Christmas tree. As had become their tradition, they opened gifts one at a time, *oohing* and *ahhing* over each. Hours later they ate a big brunch, then Ted and Meg indulged in a nap. Sasha and Dan did something much less boring: they played with their new possessions.

Late afternoon started just as nicely. The four arranged a table full of new dominoes so they'd topple one another, go up and down bridges, and ring a bell. But the dominoes kept falling before the last one was in place. Dan would accidently bump the table, the dominoes would crash, and the whole family had to start all over again. To calm a rising irritation, Ted suggested a lay-down-every-sixth-domino plan, so that any falling dominos could attack only a half dozen neighbors. Even then, no matter what they tried, they couldn't get the dominoes to fall evenly. Maybe it was the table. Maybe the surface needed to be smoother. While trying to figure out what might help, the second half of the maze collapsed. Tempers flared. Fuses blew.

Ted suggested a puzzle, a short-lived success. But just like the wayward dominoes, emotions stumbled and attacked.

"I wanted to do the edge pieces!"

"No, I was working on that part of the water."

What's wrong with our perfect day? Meg lamented. *What's the matter with us?*

———

Nothing was wrong with Ted, Meg, Sasha, or Dan. They were simply tired. Were they good when things went well and bad when things went poorly? Not at all. Early in the day they were refreshed and expectant; late in the day they were tired and spent. Christmas is anticipation. It's planning. It's intense. Few adults—let alone children—can manage that much emotion.

Once Meg figured out what was happening, she could explain it to Dan and Sasha. Recognizing their need to back off and take it easy, they made sandwiches and huddled around the TV for a Christmas video. A time of non-interaction provided the gentle togetherness they needed.

TV on Christmas? It's not that way in the picture books!

But that's the way it is in real life—after intensity, families need time to unwind. Starting with a video would have stolen family togetherness; ending with a video helped preserve it. Curling up with books would have worked similarly.

That Christmas evening showed Meg something crucial about happy days—we need to plan as creatively for down times as for exciting ones. Like John the Baptist did for Jesus, we must prepare the way for our Lord to work (Isaiah 40:3–5, Luke 3:4–6). When we plan we make it easier for our children to see God at work. And as they see Him, they can honor Him.

On that weary Christmas afternoon, Ted happened to have on hand a Christmas special he'd taped during the busy pre-Christmas days. Without it the family might have channel surfed through mindless programming. Or they might have continued to bicker, unsure of what to do with themselves and confused over why their good day ended with sad feelings. This Christmas they were lucky. Next Christmas they'll be ready.

Prepare for Picture-Perfect Holidays

Good holidays seldom just happen. That perfect morning with two sweet and thoughtful children came with planning. As God planned for creation and thus it turned out "very good," so we parents and children must plan ways to enjoy ourselves as a family (Genesis 1:31). We don't schedule every minute, or we close ourselves to spontaneity. But we prepare in ways

> **Prepare for special days in ways that bring out the good in the day and in each other**

that bring out the good in the day and in each other. We prayerfully choose special foods and prepare them. We plan how to spend the day and who we'll spend it with. We decorate, display banners, and select cards. We buy and make gifts. We do all this with an emphasis on people rather than on things. It's really true that Christmas and birthdays are just like any other days. What makes them unique is the anticipation and the events we put in them. God-guided planning makes these possible.

Planning starts with recognizing that no amount of gifts, food, commemoration, or celebration will make a day special if goodwill and love aren't already present. To make holidays happy we must cherish our children and our spouse daily. Most of us have experienced the agony of counting on ornery Uncle Chester to straighten up for Christmas, only to find him even more critical and whiny than usual. Christmas Day works no magic. The holiday's brilliance shines through only when real people choose to really care.

Unplanned happy things happen, of course. Our children win awards, good friends ask them over, and grandparents come to visit. But what makes these days happy is the caring choices and dedicated work that leads up to them. That said, let's discover ways to prepare to celebrate with our already-special families.

Enjoy the Planning

"How much longer until Christmas-Tree Day?" asked Sasha, knowing the number of days but wishing she could make them shorter by asking just one more time.

"Exactly twenty," responded Dan. "I can hardly wait!"

Meg grinned, overhearing their conversation. The day after Thanksgiving was second only to Christmas in excitement and anticipation for their children. She couldn't remember exactly when they had named it Christmas-Tree Day. They skipped the after-Thanksgiving shopping crowds to do something much more exciting: put up their Christmas tree and turn the house into a Christmas wonderland.

"We need to make our cookies to eat that day," remembered Sasha. They launched Christmas cookie season on Christmas-Tree Day.

"And we need to be sure to buy silver icicles for the tree," said Dan. "We used the last of them last year."

"Let's make a list!" Sasha urged.

"I want to help Dad put the branches on the tree!" Dan said while Sasha ran for paper. Though Meg loved real evergreens, she had long ago yielded to an artificial tree. And each year reminded her of one

MEMORY MAKERS

Little is worse than realizing you've run out of film and your children are in a classic pose—or being snowed in with nothing to do. Spell **F.A.M.I.L.Y.** to be ready for celebration on the special days and the days you decide to make special:

F*ilm and camera:* Pictures make great memories and are inexpensive to take and develop. Take photos of new haircuts, special outfits, gingerbread houses about to be eaten, school projects, giveaway gifts you wish you could keep, Christmas festivities, and birthday events. Keep at least a couple of rolls of film on hand all the time, with extra camera batteries as well.

A*ttitude of sensitivity:* Know when to take pictures and when to just enjoy the moment. Pajama pictures don't go over well with self-conscious preteens, but those same preteens might feel devastated if you forget to take the annual sitting-in-the-wrapping-paper picture. Not sure whether to snap or not? Ask.

M*anipulatives:* These are items that help families be together without the pressure of entertaining each other. We work a new puzzle every Christmas season, a diversion that became a "we always do that" tradition when we did a puzzle two years in a row. Board games, plastic models, piano music, or brainteasers work for other families. Also try stitching quilts, painting T-shirts, or whittling wood. Keep on hand whatever your family members enjoy.

MEMORY MAKERS (CONTINUED)

"I *likes*": Keep in mind the preferences of your family members as you do your routine errands. You might see everything you need for your father-in-law's favorite lasagna on sale six months before his birthday. Pop it in your freezer. When you come across a uniquely textured yarn, tuck it away for your daughter who weaves. All-year shopping spreads out the expense, makes it more likely that you'll find gifts that fit your family's personality, and heads off some of the rushed feelings of the holidays.

Little gifts: Keep on hand small stocking-stuffer type gifts that make a day special. My preschool-aged daughter once invented "Val-an-mas Day," a unique celebration that occurred during that long no-holiday stretch between Valentine's Day and Easter. Having inside information, she assured us that presents were a crucial part of the holiday. On-hand gifts equip you to celebrate Val-an-mas Days, good report cards, cooperative behavior during everybody-has-the-flu week, and much more. The few days following holidays are good times to find these gifts at half-price or less.

Yummy dessert: Even if your freezer space is limited to the top part of your refrigerator, you can stash away a pan of frosted brownies or an ice cream pie. When a special day comes, you already have a cake to celebrate with. Once you eat it, replace it within a week.

real advantage: It was fun to see the tree grow from a box of branches to a towering tree. "Wow!" somebody always said. "That's bigger than I remembered!"

Meg and Ted had first used a "Charlie Brown Christmas tree" that they paid $5 for, reduced from $18. It was so spindly they wondered if decorations would keep it from looking like green toilet brushes. But decorations did help. With pleasure they'd adorned it annually. Then when Sasha was six, Ted went on an after-Christmas shopping spree and brought home another discounted tree, the biggest and most real-looking tree Meg had ever seen. It was so enormous it barely fit in the room. "It didn't seem quite so huge in the store," Ted had said sheepishly. "But it's big enough to hold all the ornaments the kids make." And hold them it did. Ted pretended to be Scrooge at Christmas, but he was a real softy when it came to his Christmas tree. He wanted the branches just so and taught the children to assemble the tree with precision. They embraced the task with pride.

"Here's the paper! What do we need to do first?" asked Sasha.

"Well, we need to make cookies at least twice, once before Christmas-Tree Day and once afterward," said Dan.

"And we need to make our countdown chain," said Sasha. "That kind where you cut off a loop and do what it says sometime during that day. We had that store-bought one last year. I bet we can make our own this year."

"I liked all the loops except the one that said, 'Do your brother's or sister's chore for this day,'" said Dan.

"I liked that one just fine, because you got it," said Sasha quite honestly.

"Can we make the first batch of cookies this Saturday?" Dan asked Meg.

When? Meg prayed, feeling her holiday bliss squeezed by the choke of time. It was easy to think about the season, not so easy to *do* the season. *How will we find time to get ready for Christmas when we can barely keep up our regular routine?* Taking a deep breath, she reminded them that this Saturday they had several errands to run. "But why don't you put it on the following Saturday?" she suggested. "That will give me time to make room in the freezer. In the meantime you could finish listing everything you want to do this Christmas, and one of you could make a December calendar so we can see where to fit everything."

Sasha and Dan scrambled eagerly to the task. Dan made the calendar while Sasha continued the list. As Meg watched her children, she saw them "live in order to please God" (1 Thessalonians 4:1). They cooperated, encouraged each other, focused on celebrating Christ's birth. Their joy as they planned this happy event was simply wonderful.

"I want to read that Christmas book we found half-price after Christmas last year," said Sasha. "I've been waiting all year to find out what it's about."

"I can hardly wait to see our other Christmas books, too," agreed Dan.

Ted had tucked the Christmas books in with the Christmas tree one year while packing the ornaments. The children so enjoyed rediscovering them that it had become an annual tradition. It seemed like many of their traditions had started that way: Do it once, enjoy it, then repeat it on purpose. Meg also liked the way their nativity sets had multiplied. Ted and Meg had painted a ceramic set before the children were born. Toddler Dan had a simple plastic one to play with. Later both children had made a large wooden one with their grandparents. And other nativity sets would likely join this unintentional, but most enjoyed, collection.

"Can we get out all the nativity sets rather than just one of them?" asked Sasha, as though reading Meg's mind. "I could figure out where to put each one."

"I think that would be great. Put it on your list so we won't forget," said Meg. "And if you have ideas on where to put them, write that too."

"Do you have advent calendars for us?" asked Sasha. "I liked the ones where we scratched off the silver stuff to get to the pictures. The little door ones are okay too. I just want one that tells a story—not just pictures behind each door."

Meg agreed. "That's what advent is, looking forward to Christ's coming. So it makes more sense to pick a calendar that tells little bits of His story every day." Meg much preferred teaching about God through the course of the day than sitting down for a special session. It reminded both her and her children that God is a part of daily life. She thanked God for this bit of inspiration.

"I remember when I was in first grade and read the Christmas story from the advent calendar on Christmas day," said Dan. "That one was just like Luke 2."

"It was Luke 2 just broken into little bits," said Sasha with authority.

"And in answer to your question, yes I have new advent calendars," said Meg. "But I don't have a new Christmas cookie cutter yet. Would you write that on your list, and on my shopping list?"

"Sure," said Dan. "And what about Mrs. Aaron? We always get her something since she lives alone."

"I want to make her a gift," said Sasha. "I'll get out my weaving loom right now. She liked what I wove last year."

"That would be great," said Meg. "Every time you feel like you can't wait a minute longer for Christmas-Tree Day, weave a few rows for Mrs. Aaron.

"Then it will be like it's already here," said Sasha.

"Exactly," said Meg. This is how they'd get it all done. They'd spread it out and do a few rows at a time.

Adapt Meg's Timetable

After supper Dan and Sasha were eager to decide who would do what, and when. But Meg knew she'd do these more patiently earlier in the day and earlier in the week. Tonight's fatigue would make it harder for her to think clearly or make wise choices. "Put your initials next to the things you want to do," she suggested, "and we'll make plans tomorrow."

"But which ones do you want, Mama?" asked Sasha.

"I'm tired tonight so it's hard for me to decide right now. I'd like to make my choices tomorrow," said Meg. She purposely admitted her weariness rather than let her children think she wasn't interested in them or in their Christmas list. When they knew the reasons for her actions they were more willing to wait.

The children went to work.

"No! You get to do the branch-putting-on. You can't do the spreading too!" argued Sasha a few minutes later.

"Dan and Sasha, we're not deciding it all tonight," reminded Meg. "You're just writing what you want to do. If you both want to do the same thing, you can both write your initials there. We might figure out a way for each of you to do it, or we can divide the 'most wants' between you."

"About five more minutes and you need to start your baths," Meg said a few minutes later, to keep her children from thinking they were going to bed for arguing. Meg wasn't the only one wearing down after a long day.

The next morning Sasha and Dan went off to school reluctantly, preferring to stay home and make Christmas plans. But Meg promised they could work on the plans right after school.

Most years Dan and Sasha waited until after Thanksgiving to plan. But they were interested early this year. So Meg tailored the process to their needs. Maybe they'd find time to do more this way. Other years they'd be further behind in planning, and would do less.

With the freshness of the morning, Meg caught her children's excitement. Treating herself to a few minutes of fun before diving into the day's tasks, she looked over their lists and added her thoughts:

Get the boxes from the attic.
Make menus.
Buy ingredients for Christmas baking.

Meg marveled at her children's creative ideas. Reading their ornament ideas, Meg remembered Ted lifting up tiny Sasha to put the final ornament on top of the tree. Now quite able to reach the top herself, she still begs him to lift her and zoom in for the closing adornment. *Those are the moments that make the preparation more than worthwhile*, Meg recognized with satisfaction. These Christmas treasures are more than just memories for Meg's family. They bind her family together and build a foundation of security that reaches into every area of life. Because she, Ted, Sasha, and Dan have shared good holidays, each day brings special trust and family connection.

Armed with new motivation to do Christmas, Meg dove into the day's deadlines, lest she make the calendar out all by herself. When Sasha and Dan returned from school, they rapidly completed their homework while Meg put the finishing touches on the project that was due the next morning. Then the three eagerly began calendar creating. They divided things up by interest and ability.

"I'll give you the branch arranging if I can put the lights on myself this year," bargained Sasha.

CHRISTMAS TREASURES

Each year find a new way to make Christmas special. Let this list spur your own ideas, uniquely created for your own God-honoring family:

Discover your own ways to honor Jesus: Though every day is to be a celebration of Christ's coming, Christmas provides extra focus. See it as His day as you plan each portion. Discover ways Jesus wants you to honor Him with it. Make your main dessert a birthday cake for Jesus. Let the sparkle of decorations remind you to be His light in the world. Let your advent calendar give you a Bible portion to live that day. Treat each other as you would treat Jesus.

Make your own stockings: Cut out little felt shapes of each family member's favorite interests and collections. One child's stocking might include a computer, a teddy bear, a book, and more. Another child's stocking might display a model train, a horse, footprints (for enjoying bare feet), and more. Sew the shapes onto a red stocking with a beading needle, sequins, and seed beads. Some families add a new item each year and date the year that item was added. This records changing interests and becomes a cherished history.

Open an advent calendar: In addition to the 24-little-doors-to-open advent calendar, there are scratch-off ones, color-a-picture-each-day ones, and those from which you daily read a tiny book that tells a portion of the Christmas story. This daily bit of fun makes it easier to wait for the big day and to focus on Jesus' coming.

Build your own menu: There's nothing sacred about turkey and dressing for Thanksgiving, nor ham and sweet potatoes for Christmas. Your family might prefer homemade pizza for Christmas breakfast and scrambled eggs for supper. Make your celebration unique!

CHRISTMAS TREASURES (CONTINUED)

Choose your own timetable: There's no one right way to honor Jesus at Christmas. If you thrive on crowds and feel energized by the last-minute rush, by all means enjoy it. If shopping all year gives you the warmth of gifts being safely tucked away and the enjoyment of buying special gifts when you see them, shop all year. If you like midnight services and sleeping late, participate in those worship services. If you're an early riser, choose a dawn worship. If five nativity sets confuse rather than multiply your joy in Jesus, use a different one each year. Do whatever gives you and your family the time together, the joy of giving, and the peace to treasure the season.

Set your own traditions: Determine at least one way you'll give non-material gifts at Christmas and on birthdays. Maybe you tell each other something you like about them, or you each recall a favorite Christmas memory.

Start a new book: Find a new Christmas book to read together during the season. Even if it's just a couple pages a day, this cozy activity adds calmness to the craziness of the season. Keep each year's book with the Christmas ornaments, so everyone can review the books each year. Some years you might discover two or three new Christmas books; other years none. So save up the extras for the lean years. Inside each book write the year you read it.

Read Scripture: For each of the four weeks before Christmas, try family devotions on passages related to Christ's coming. Consider lighting an advent wreath while reading and sharing, one candle for each of four weekly themes: Hope, Peace, Joy, and Love. Advent guides with Scripture and devotions are available through churches or bookstores. Let each family member take a turn reading passages and questions.

"It's a deal," agreed Dan.

"One thing I don't want to do is get stuck with the dishes again this year," insisted Sasha.

"Me either," agreed Dan again.

"Then who do you propose to do them?" asked Meg.

"You and Dad!" they suggested in unison.

"Wrong!" said Meg. "Now that just the jobs nobody wants remain, let's divide those like the others. Nobody likes dishwashing, or putting the ornament boxes back after we put up the tree, or vacuuming up the messes. Nobody likes gathering and taking out the wrapping paper trash. But it's got to be done."

"Why can't you and Dad just do it?" said Dan.

"Because everybody has less chores when we all do a few. Parents don't like chores any more than kids do," explained Meg.

"I'll take out the trash," said Dan, rapidly choosing the least dreaded of the tasks, lest he be left with something worse.

"And I'll put the boxes back after we put up the tree," said Sasha.

"I'll repack the ornaments after Christmas, if you'll get the icicles off the branches," offered Dan.

"I can handle that," said Sasha.

"But what about the dishes after Christmas baking and feasting?" said Meg.

Silence.

"How about we take turns," Meg suggested. "We have the biggest bunch of dishes after Christmas Eve supper and the next biggest after New Year's Day. Each of you take one of those and Dad or I will pair up with you."

"Then we'll alternate for the baking days," said Sasha with a hint of willingness. "But can you wash the table, Mom? I never can get it clean after we've iced and decorated cookies."

"Yes, I can do that. And I'll vacuum the kitchen on those days too," Meg agreed, wanting to get all the sugar up before it was tracked through the house.

"If we play Christmas carols or pair up, the dishwashing won't be quite so bad," agreed Dan reluctantly. "I want to wash with Dad."

"Me too!" said Sasha.

"Can we trade on the pairing too?" asked Dan.

"Certainly," affirmed Meg. "Now some things have to be done on certain days. If we don't bake cookies before Thanksgiving, we can't eat cookies on Thanksgiving. When do we have our first cookie baking?"

"Next weekend," said Dan.

"And that means we have to have our ingredients before then," said Meg. "Who will get out the recipes and make the list?"

"I will," said Dan. "But how will I know if we need it or not? We usually have flour."

"Write it down anyway and I'll decide," said Meg. "Be sure to put how much we need of each thing. Like for two cookie recipes just tally all eight cups of flour on the same line. It would be better to have too much than too little. Then while we're running errands tomorrow, I'll get the ingredients."

"We need to start the advent calendars on December 1," said Sasha. "I'll write that on November 30. Can we get them out now?"

"Not yet," said Meg. "That would take some of the fun from the first day. Remember how much you enjoy looking at the calendar for the first time?" Meg felt like the big bad wolf when she made her kids wait. But she felt worse when the fun was flattened because she gave in.

"We need to have teacher and friend gifts picked and wrapped by the day of the school party," said Dan. "And our family gifts wrapped before Christmas Eve!"

"Right. Put that down about a week before the party day," said Meg. "I'm glad we got so many gifts at after-Christmas sales last year."

"Yeah, my friends are going to love those Christmas teddy bears," recalled Sasha. "I can hardly wait to open that box."

"It'll be great," said Meg. "We still need to buy a few things, so be watching while we're out."

"We need to put the church's hanging-of-the-greens on that first Sunday in December," said Sasha. "I think that's when it is."

"I think you're right, but let's pencil it until we hear for certain," said Meg. "Most of the other things we can do on any day. We'll choose one to do each day of December, to make each day special. Remember our Christmas story last year? You said you wanted to do something special each day like that family did. Maybe we can pick from your list, taking turns choosing."

"Yeah, then it would be a surprise what each day would bring," said Sasha.

"I like that too," said Dan. "Can I pick first?"

"Why don't we let Dad pick first," said Meg. "We can wonder all day what it will be and when he comes home we'll all do it together."

"Yeah!" said Dan. "If I can wait that long."

"And will you surprise us some too, Mom?" said Sasha. "I like your new ideas, ones we've never tried before."

"Thanks, Sasha," said Meg, pleased at such a spontaneous compliment. "I'll see what I can do." Meg had found some candles that burn down to reveal surprises. Maybe that would be a good first surprise. But how would she make them Christmassy? Well, that would come.

"I think we've got it all," said Sasha. "Anything else?"

"What about the end of Christmas Day, when we're tired and spent? What would give us a time of cozy togetherness?" asked Meg.

"We watched Christmas videos last year," said Dan.

"We could read a new Christmas book," added Sasha. "You usually give us a book for Christmas."

> Christmas is a together celebration, not a show we put on for our children.

"Glad you mentioned that," said Meg, not realizing she usually did this. "I'll be sure to get two new chapter books especially for Christmas evening. We'll open them that night."

"That would be even better than a video," said Dan.

"Let's post the calendar and list on the refrigerator," said Meg. "And I'll copy some of these things into my own calendar."

"Oh, I can't wait! Can't we do just one thing today?" urged Dan.

"Well, we've done our calendar. What about making the countdown chain? You can cut the strips and write the good deeds on each one," suggested Meg.

"Then can we put it together?" asked Dan.

"If you still have time and energy, that would be great," said Meg. "Don't you love Christmas?"

Make It a Together Celebration

Christmas isn't an event to put on for your children, but a celebration to involve every member of the family. Doing Christmas together means we don't have to outgrow it or mourn because someone didn't appreciate our efforts enough. It's a together thing, a web of giving and of receiving each other's unique offerings. Each family member matters in the preparation for and celebration of Christ's birth.

In a life-changing way, Christmas and other holidays are the laboratory for learning how to celebrate—each person discovers ways to put in effort and yield relaxation and joy. You prepare the way for a together celebration when you build a team as Meg did. Ask your children's help with worship ideas, picking presents, menu choosing, and activity selections. Custom design the responsibilities to the personality and age of your child. Even two-year-olds can help stuff stockings and put the bows on the gifts. Your five-year-old may not be able to keep a secret, but she can arrange the presents under the tree or place the nativity sets. Your preteen who wants to hear everything that's said or experienced might chronicle the holiday with a dated Christmas journal, including interviews with family members. Your teenager might not get into cookie baking, but he could bake a grand turkey or guide a worship celebration.

Offer yourself to your children, rather than ask that they always help you. Be the one who holds the finger for the bow, who gets the ingredients out while your child stirs, who washes dishes and sets the table while your teenagers work on dinner. Your example of servant love will encourage your children to offer the same to each other.

Planning together isn't just important, it's fun. I'm convinced that children enjoy the planning as much as the big day. When they could barely toddle, our girls were stashing surprises and wrapping treats to give to cousins. Why save the joy of giving for ourselves? Involvement with planning stretches out the fun of the holiday while teaching the joy of giving to others in Jesus' name. Purposely include each member in the planning and then jointly enjoy the fruits of all the family's labors.

Your children's involvement will prompt you to keep a people perspective during the special day. If Dan wants to savor each gift, waiting awhile to open his other gifts, so be it. If Sasha prefers scrambled eggs to roasted ham, choose that for your feast (it's easier to make and produces fewer dishes!). But if Sasha wants to rip open her presents and Dan wants ham, balance the needs of both family members to make the day go well. Maybe you'll allow up to ten minutes between presents. Perhaps you'll serve green eggs and ham.

People-focus is not selfish. It's loving each other in Jesus' name. Your children aren't the center of the day—Jesus is. In His honor, free each family member to focus on the others. Prompt cooperation, coordination, and care. Encourage each family member to plan and celebrate with your specific family in mind. Storybooks, magazine articles, even your own expectations can spoil the day if you don't focus on the people God has given you.

Joy Tip

Wonderful holidays don't just happen. We've got to plan for them. Jump in with both feet to prepare for your holidays, convinced that the swim is as fun as the finish line.

6

A HO-HUM EXISTENCE WITH SCATTERED HIGHS AND LOWS

Whatever you do, work at it with all your heart, as working for the Lord, not for men.

—Colossians 3:23

"I hate it when Christmas is over," said Ben Spencer as he glumly took the ornaments off of the tree.

"Me too," agreed his brother, Greg. "Everything gets so busy again."

"It is kind of sad," their father Jared said. "Our Christmas pace is wonderful—we're off school and work. We're together for extra worship. We have entire afternoons of relaxed puzzle-working."

"Yes, but routine has its own relaxation," added their mother, Cathy. "Like an hour to read every night before bed. It's been a couple weeks since we've had that. We've been so busy every night that you've had only a few minutes of reading at most."

"But I like traveling and staying up late," said Gina.

"Me too," Cathy agreed, aware that voicing the sadness is one of the best ways to move on through it. "Maybe after we get the tree put away we can write down some of our favorite things about this Christmas season. We bought that Christmas journal but haven't written much in it."

"I want to write about the Christmas custard," said Greg. "It took forever to make, but the taste was worth the work. I want to add that to our Christmas baking list for next year."

"And I like that present-a-day idea," said Ben. Jared's mother had

93

Birthday Party Themes

The next special occasion in your home might be a birthday. You can add to the anticipation, spread out the fun, and beat birthday party boredom with *themes*. The following themes can span many years with a bit of adaptation. Choose decorations, invitations, icebreakers, and party games that match your theme. Remember tried-and-trues like charades, decorate-your-own-party bag, and musical chairs:

Teddy Bear Picnic: Each child brings his favorite teddy bear. Sit on a picnic blanket spread across the floor. Stuff, sew shut, and decorate pre-assembled teddy bears for an icebreaker. Eat teddy-bear shaped cake and decorate ice cream with teddy-bear shaped cookies. Play games with teddy bear partners.

Princess Party: Everyone comes dressed as a princess (adapt to princes for guys). For an icebreaker make your own crown with precut forms and an assortment of markers, stick-on jewels, and glue. Play charades with fairy tale names and characters. Develop a trivia game about real-life royalty. Admire each costume and hear the story behind it.

Hero Party: Guests come dressed as Super-heroes or sports figures. The icebreaker is to draw a comic strip of your character. Games include balloon volleyball and other adaptations of ball games that equalize ability.

Me 'n' My Pet: Guests bring a stuffed animal and dress themselves to match. Crack a piñata shaped like a favorite pet. Guess the animal that matches the paw print. Specify "stuffed" when you ask guests to bring a pet.

BIRTHDAY PARTY THEMES (CONTINUED)

Mystery Party: Send invitations cut into puzzle pieces. Use brainteasers for icebreakers, and play games with an element of mystery. Consider playing Clue™ in its original, museum, and video versions.

Zoo Party: Come dressed as a zoo animal. Generate a crossword puzzle of zoo animals on your computer as an icebreaker. Challenge guests to create their own animal from dough, foil, or pipe cleaners. Combine them to form a menagerie. Name the kind of habitat each imaginary animal would need. In place of cake, guests model, bake, ice, and eat their own cookie dough dessert.

Makeover Madness: Twelve-year-old girls love this one. Invite a make-up consultant to teach the girls about make-up and to give each a facial and makeover. Suggest that she bring order forms that the girls can fill out and take home. Plan to order cosmetics yourself or otherwise pay her for her time.

Model Creation: Invite each guest to bring a new put-together model, perhaps related to a specific theme. Assemble them during the party, sharing tips for model success. Or build one large model for the birthday child to keep. Party favors might be mini-models or small construction sets.

Bible Challenge Celebration: Guests bring their favorite Bible verse written on a card. Collect these as they arrive and set them aside. Play a Bible scavenger hunt icebreaker. Then guess each other's favorite verses and why they like that verse. Play games with a Bible theme. Serve foods named in the Bible.

sent all her stocking stuffers wrapped and numbered. She suggested they open one a day for the twelve days before Christmas to spread out the fun. It had been a grand success, especially the season-oriented gifts. Gina could wear her Christmas earrings more than one day, and Ben could use his Christmas pencils at school. That tradition was definitely worth repeating.

"What's the next holiday?" asked Gina.

"Greg's birthday," Cathy said. "It's not for another month but it's not too early to start thinking about a theme."

"But I don't have a theme idea this year," said Greg. "What do you think?"

"There are all kinds of possibilities," said Cathy. "Costume themes, mystery themes, stuff-to-make themes. You can look through the birthday book. Whatever you pick, remember to choose an icebreaker to get your friends comfortable with each other, and some party games to play after the gifts and cake."

"Can we go ahead and write ideas for favors and draw a picture of how I want my cake to be?" asked Greg, ready to plan for the next event.

"Sure," said Jared. "But first we've got to get this tree packed and the ornaments put away."

After Christmas there's always a little sadness at the Spencer house. It's not that the presents are over, though they do feel a bit of the "material-things-just-can't-satisfy" letdown. It's not that the lights come down, though they do miss the glitter and gala. What makes them most sad is having to leave behind the level of togetherness they feel at Christmas. All five Spencers kick back and enjoy each other with a luxury not readily available during any other time of year. It happens partly because everyone expects them to be home with their family during the Christmas holidays—even Ronald McDonald stays home on Christmas Day. But it happens more because the Spencers designate those as days off. The children turn down activities with friends to be home. Hardworking Dad and Mom relax during the Christmas holidays and take time to do the activities they don't otherwise feel free to do. As much as the Spencers like their rest-of-the-year routines, they grieve at returning to the busyness of them.

Moving from big events to routine ones is at the root of daily living. And growing from those roots are the sweet experiences of savoring the present. An attitude of meeting each day with joy makes it easier to move past the holidays. And holidays become even richer because children learn there's more to life than the out-of-the-ordinary events. There's happiness in simple things.

So should we just bite the bullet and swallow our sadness after holidays? Should we assume that Christians won't feel let down? Not at all. Enjoying life with our children doesn't mean constant grins and no tears. Sometimes it means crying together. Sometimes it means walking through grief. Always it means caring about each other enough to hear and understand whatever the other is feeling. And rather than wallowing in the melancholy, it means taking action to heal it and move together to the next events of life.

Give a Little Down Time

Christmas isn't the only day that launches a letdown feeling. A birthday, sleepover, church retreat—any special time—finds sadness on its heels. Remember Elijah, who singlehandedly stood against 450 Baal bullies while God put them in their place? (1 Kings 18–19). It was an ecstatic time for Elijah. God mightily demonstrated His power. Elijah was on top of the world.

But the next day was a different story. After triumphing over hundreds of pagan prophets, Elijah faced the wrath of one woman named Jezebel. How did brave Elijah react? He ran for his life. In despair he begged God to kill him and end his miserable existence. Why the change from nobody-can-stop-me triumph to my-life-is-a-terrible-mess sadness? Elijah was physically and spiritually exhausted. What was God's prescription? Rest, food, and friendship.

Certainly it must be more complex than that. But it's not. The simple things make the biggest difference during times of sadness. Elijah felt his sadness, voiced it to God, and took the action God recommended.

We families can follow this same prescription: notice sad feelings, encourage our children to voice them, and recommend actions to heal that sadness. Often all that's needed is a little down time to rest and eat, followed by the loving care of family members.

"I'm so homesick for Granddaddy," said Greg the week after

PLACES TO PARTY

Some families prefer birthday party locations other than home. They can allow larger groups or different activities—it's hard to roller skate in most living rooms:

Fast-food restaurant: Preschoolers like these simple but exciting locations. Some fast-food restaurants provide the party hostess, meal, cake, favors, and party games for a set price per child.

Costumed character restaurant: Children under four years old can be terrified of *Chimpee* or *Chuck E. Cheese*, so don't invite a scary situation by using this location for children too young to enjoy it. But for older kids this can be an evening to remember.

Roller skating rink or ice skating rink: Skating is the entertainment; you bring the cake and ice cream. Use bright name tags to better keep an eye on your partygoers. Even better, combine with a cousin or friend to rent the whole rink. Then you'll know all the children are yours.

Party room: Pizza places and other restaurants often provide a private room at no charge if you order their food. This is good for older children and young teens who need more space than an average living room but want to choose and prepare their own games. Order generously and clean up well afterward.

Miniature golf, bowling, or other sport activity: Choose a place that allows much interaction between children. Being together, not entertaining, is the goal of birthday parties.

Museum adventure: Many museums and nature centers offer birthday party packages that include exploring the museum, learning about computers, meeting animals, and more. Check your local phone book.

Christmas. He had spent the weekend with his grandfather and was now unpacking. "At the same time I was really ready to come home. I got homesick for here. How come?"

"You like both places," Cathy said, pushing back her urge to make everything instantly okay. "It's nice to have two places you feel so at home. But it's hard not to be able to be at both places at once."

"Yeah, it is," said Greg. He felt better knowing that his feelings made sense. But he still felt sad.

"And it's normal to feel a little sad after a very happy time," continued Cathy. "Just relax this afternoon. Read. Write. Talk with God."

Greg spent a little extra time in his room, a little extra time just thinking and remembering.

Cathy wanted to whisk away her son's sadness with, "You'll feel better soon" or "Don't be lonely." But to do so would discredit Greg and his feelings. Instead, she gave Greg the gift of grieving, the gift of time. She didn't push him to talk but purposely stayed available for when he was ready to speak.

She didn't have to wait long.

"Is the computer free? I think I'll draw a picture for Granddaddy," said Greg brightly after he'd been in his room for a while.

"Good idea," Cathy said. "He's probably feeling a little lonely for you too. The picture will make him feel closer to you. What are you going to put in your picture?"

"I'm not sure yet. I'm thinking about us in the workshop. We did some serious sanding down there," said Greg. "It was fun."

"Sounds like it," said Cathy. "I'm glad God gave you such great grandparents."

Greg had felt his sadness, voiced it, felt it some more, and now was taking action to heal it. Greg's grief, a letdown after a very happy time with his grandparent, took only a day or so. Some griefs, like losing a grandparent to death, take much longer. But the process is the same: feel it, voice it, feel it some more, take action. Sometimes the voicing means asking a question; other times it means telling your memories. Sometimes the action means resting, making a gift, taking a walk, writing a song, returning to school and chores. In all cases, the feeling, the voicing, and the acting are a time to remember the past and readjust to routine life. (My book *Will I Ever Feel Good Again?* is a guided journal that helps children and youth understand their feelings of grief and find a path through them. You can give it as a gift, or study it with a group to discover ways to care.)

Greg has similar mournful feelings every time he comes home from his grandparents' house and every time something fun comes to an end. He and his siblings use these voices and actions:

- Write about the happy event to relive the fun. After Christmas is a good time to do a Christmas journal.
- Write a letter to someone who matters in the event: "You made the church retreat special to me by."
- Compose a melody or song about the event, how you felt then, how you feel now.
- Talk with a family member about what happened and how you feel about it.
- Listen to a family member talk about how she/he feels about it.
- Paint, draw, or doodle.
- Bake, hike, exercise, or otherwise physically express yourself.
- Watch home videos or look at pictures of the person.
- Begin planning the next event.
- Talk with God while doing all the above.

Both the joys and the griefs of life are equally important. Refuse to miss either of these. Pushing sadness aside forces it to keep bobbing to the surface like a cork pushed under the water. The best way past sadness is to pick it up, hold it for a while, and then do with it as God instructs. Move right through the middle of sadness to find the happiness on the other side.

Move on Through the Sadness

For Greg the path through sadness and back to routine life is straightforward and clearly expressed. Gina has more difficulty. As a younger child with a different temperament, she finds it harder to pinpoint her feelings. Her sadness shows as irritability and orneriness. She snaps at everyone and then wonders why her brothers fight with her. Cathy approaches Gina a bit differently than Greg.

"Gina, your behavior has been pretty mean today. There's bound to be a good reason for that. Can you tell me what's going on?" offered Cathy.

"I'm fine! What's the big deal?" responded Gina. "Aren't I entitled to a bad mood once in a while?"

"Certainly. But you can't treat your brothers badly just because you feel badly," Cathy insisted. "And you have to talk more kindly to me. I'm wondering if you're feeling jealous because Greg's birthday is coming up and yours won't be for another six months."

"I'm not jealous!" Gina contended. "I'm just in a bad mood."

"Well, there's always a reason for bad moods—you're jealous, tired, disappointed, confused, guilty, or something else. Whatever the reason, why don't you get your watercolors and go outside for a while? Find something you'd like to paint."

"I'm not in the mood," said Gina. "And like I said—nothing is wrong with me."

"You may not be in the mood to paint now, but once you start painting you'll probably get in the mood," said Cathy.

"I don't have any ideas," responded Gina.

"The ideas will come. And while you have some alone-time painting you can sort out your feelings. Invite God along on the sorting. He can help you figure out what to do. Maybe all you need is that time alone. Maybe you need to talk to Dad or me about it. Maybe you need to take action to repair a wrong or do a right."

"I guess painting would be okay. But what should I paint?" asked Gina hesitantly.

"Oh, I don't know. Look around to see what's outside. Or you can think about the events of the last few days—school, home, church, free time. What's been happening and how do you feel about it?" suggested Cathy. "While you paint, think and pray."

Gina went out reluctantly but came back in refreshed. Cathy never found out exactly what was bothering Gina that day. But Gina found a path through her misery.

Sometimes our kids will share their inner feelings with us; sometimes not. But in both cases, our children can share their feelings with God. And in all cases we can offer actions and words that lead back to contentment. If we allow our children to stay mired in their misery, we steal time and joy from them. Let the feelings do their job—show what's right or wrong, point to the action that needs doing. Then prompt your children to do that action and move on. Different from whisking away difficulties, this process moves us through life at the pace God directs.

Make the Routine Marvelous

One of the best ways to make the transition from big events to not-so-big ones is to make each day special. The problem with this is that most days are neither desperately sad nor ecstatically exciting. They're routine. So are we doomed to a ho-hum existence with scattered highs and lows? Not at all. Contrary to popular opinion, routine life is anything but dull. There's much to celebrate in each new day. If we assume that days have to be exceptional to be fun, we miss most of life. We can find magnificence in the mundane. All we have to do is pay attention and know where to look.

Begin by rejecting the notion that routine equals boring. Routine can give us the good we want: dinner together, an hour to read in the evening, telling about the events of the day, church participation, exercise through organized sports or casual walks. These events punctuate the paragraphs of our lives.

> Pushing sadness aside forces it to keep bobbing to the surface like a cork pushed under the water. The best way past sadness is to pick it up, hold it for a while, and then do with it as God instructs.

Notice the richness in each of your daily experiences. Cathy Spencer puts it this way, "When I'm paying attention I recognize the advantage of each part of our day. The hustle-bustle of getting ready in the morning gives us opportunity to ease into the day. All three of my children wake up gradually so we start with the simple things—getting dressed, and then breakfast. We do hair and decisions when they're fully awake.

"During this time I can offer each child a word of encouragement for the day ahead. Perhaps Gina has a book report, Greg has a new friend he's shy about talking to, and Ben fears dropping fly balls during the recess baseball game. In addition to encouraging them on these challenges, I help them focus on the good in that day. Gina has computer on Tuesdays and she loves that. Greg has math challenge, and Ben has library. And then I prompt them to look for the blessings we don't know about yet.

"When they get home, we take time to hear each other's stories over an afternoon snack. That sharing time is repeated when Jared comes in from work. Bedtime brings unwinding and reading. We all five snuggle in to the truth that we're loved in this home.

"These pockets of togetherness come in the midst of extremely hectic days. On Tuesdays the children get home at 3:30, must be at piano at 4:00, and then Greg and I drive to speech therapy by 6:00. We do homework in the car on those days, quizzing while the others are in lessons. And that's one of three nights a week we can't eat supper together. It's crazy, but the routine helps us do all the things we want to do."

Cathy highlights a tough family problem: Most families are so bombarded with school projects, homework, and ball practices that even tidbits of togetherness are tough to come by. But look a little closer: Could the school project bring the satisfaction of a job well done? Could the homework—at least some of it—give exactly the practice your child needs to master mathematics? And could the soccer games provide opportunity for your child to work as a team, and for you to cheer your child in public?

It's not a simple formula. The good that results from an activity doesn't mean it deserves a spot in your schedule. And being busy doesn't necessarily mean you need to drop something. So if more isn't better and less isn't better, what's the formula for a good routine? It's a matter of looking at each routine event to decide if it works toward God's joy. Together with God determine if your days are just full of activity, or if they bring God's kingdom.

Jesus asked that God's "kingdom come" and God's "will be done" (Matthew 6:10). Are your routine activities accomplishing this? Do they bring the "love, joy, peace, patience, kindness, goodness, faithfulness, gentleness, and self-control" that enable you to "do it all for the glory of God?" (Galatians 5:22–23; 1 Corinthians 10:31). Do they help others understand and live for God? If so, they will bring your family refreshment and joy. They will bring good to the people you encounter.

This doesn't mean you'll have automatic refreshment or that you'll feel giddy instantly. Both Cathy and Greg dread Greg's speech therapy on Tuesday nights. It's a grueling reminder that Greg has hearing loss, must struggle to hear each conversation, and must work six times harder to learn to speak clearly. Both Greg and Cathy are bone tired afterward. But weekly they continue to contribute two and a half hours to this pursuit—ninety minutes of driving and an hour of therapy. Why? Because the hours, and weeks, and months of work make it possible for Greg to listen well, to speak articulately, and to use those skills to build friendships. These friendships demonstrate God's love and motivate those friends to relate lovingly to other friends.

As each friendship grows, kindness and goodness replace selfishness and suspicion. God's kingdom comes and God's will is done (Matthew 6:10). And Greg finds the long-term refreshment of knowing "It is God who arms me with strength and makes my way perfect. He makes my feet like the feet of a deer; he enables me to stand on the heights" (2 Samuel 22:33–34). Because of Greg's expressed devotion, people around Greg thirst for God "like a deer pants for streams of water" (Psalm 42:1).

Take a close look at the activities that spend the precious hours in your family's day. Are they the activities God would choose? Every time one person obeys God in an action or a word, we grow a little closer to God's perfect kingdom. We experience a clearer picture of what God's will really is. Do your activities and your rests from activities do this? You'll likely find your choices between good and better, rather than between good and bad.

Evaluating your routine means making hard choices. One spring Gina became interested in a ballet/jazz class. Her best friend had invited her to join, her hero was a gifted dancer, and after she tried a sample class, Gina fell madly in love with dance. There was one small problem—the dance class met on the one free evening her family had. They used that Thursday afternoon to complete big school projects, to catch up from all the week's running, and to go to bed a bit earlier after Wednesday night church. But Gina wanted to take dance so badly she could taste it. She begged and begged.

"I won't get too tired!" she pleaded. "I'm the one in our family who has more trouble with getting bored than with too much to do."

"I know, Gina," answered Cathy with a heavy heart. "But we simply don't have the time to spend. We need this free evening for schoolwork, for dreaming and creating. Maybe next year we can rearrange our schedule some. But this year things are set. Besides, the class has already started. You'd feel behind."

"No I wouldn't!" Gina insisted. "Lu has promised to help me

catch up. We've already been practicing. And the teacher says I'm a quick learner. She says I'll be dancing right along with the class in no time."

"It's hard, Gina, but we just can't do it right now," said Cathy.

"Is it money? I'll help pay. I think I have enough for the shoes," Gina offered. "Please, Mom, I've never wanted to do anything so badly in all my life."

"I believe you," said Cathy honestly. "And I hate to tell you no, but I must. We just don't have the day to give it. I will keep it on the top of my list for this fall."

"But fall is years away!" Gina lamented. "By then Lu will have moved up and I'll be in the class behind her."

"That may be," said Cathy. "And then you'd have to decide if you want to start a bit behind her. I want you to have the dance class that you want, but we just can't do it this year. I have to preserve your free afternoon and evening."

Gina continued to push. And each time Cathy's heart hurt. But not as much as the out-every-night-with-no-time-off exhaustion. All family members would have suffered if no one had any time to rest. For Gina's sake and for the family's sake, Cathy had to hold firm. It was agonizingly difficult, but it paid generous dividends in a manageable pace of life.

> Be a miner of real riches. Miners recognize the real jewels, not just the shiny stones.

Several weeks later Cathy brought up the dance class: "Gina, I know you still want to take the dance class, and I'm proud of the way you're waiting," she complimented.

"Thanks, Mom," said Gina. She had learned a bit of patience as her mom helped her choose what was best.

Be a miner of real riches. Miners recognize the real jewels, not just the shiny stones. Make choices that control your routine rather than letting your routine control you. Carve out time for the events that matter most and preserve those events. Serving at the seasonal deacon dinner is a good cause, but you may need to say no in order to help your daughter do a research project. Let your routine lead you to see the delight in the simple, and the simple delights in each other.

MAKE MAGNIFICENT THE MUNDANE

It's the little things that make routine days marvelous. To consciously bring joy to each day:

Smile . . .

In the pressure to get everything done, we parents frown a lot. Deliberately smile at your children to communicate your interest and genuine love.

Say "I like being with you" . . .

In 100 variations. Here are three to get you started: "You're a treat to parent"; "Life is more fun with you in it"; "I love your persistent perspective."

Value what's valuable . . .

Be as captivated by the caterpillar on the stick as your child is. Sing along with your child rather than give in to self-consciousness. Hear and understand your child's viewpoints. Applaud your child's Christlikeness. Cherish your child's loving choices.

Notice . . .

Pay attention to your child and to God. What good is your child doing? How is God working in her and you to bring about that good? What neat treats from God are both of you enjoying today: the sunshine? the rain? the closeness of your family?

Enjoy Christian music . . .

While riding in the car together, while doing chores, while getting ready in the morning, play Christian music. Let the music prompt your children toward good, help them understand what's right and why, enhance conversation, and give times of comfortable togetherness. Choose songs with words that do all this and more. Christian music can be bouncy or soft, loud or quiet. It's the words that count.

MAKE MAGNIFICENT THE MUNDANE (CONTINUED)

Use kind words . . .

Rather than snap when you're tired (or allow your children to do so), speak kindly. "I'm really feeling grouchy. Please give me just a minute to calm down." Or if you're angry, say so directly, "What you did made me mad because it hurt your brother" rather than "Why do you do such mean things?" Simple kindness makes the day. So guide yourself and your children to be consistently kind in word and attitude.

Call mishaps adventures rather than catastrophes . . .

Your attitude will be contagious. If you whine about the flat tire, your children will too. But if you joke about going to rescue Daddy from the fire-breathing flat tire, your children will find adventure in the inconveniences.

Laugh . . .

Learn to laugh with your children, not at them. Grow the art of teasing that never puts down but instead helps everyone feel a part of the group. (See "Family Funnies" in Chapter 3 for ideas.) Enjoy life and encourage your children to do so also.

Take time apart . . .

Enjoying your children does not mean continual togetherness. We all need time alone and apart. My mother used to sit on the back porch each evening after it got dark. As a teenager I joined her, thinking she needed company. I now understand that time was her time to think through the day and unwind before resting. I'm now the mother. I need the conversation to cease so I can refuel for the next day of happy hubbub. Explain this to your children and give all family members the private time they need to thrive on togetherness.

Add Cheer to the Chore

Chores form one of the biggest barriers to enjoying routine life. Most children (even we grown-up ones) assume chore time means misery. It doesn't have to. Work can be as fun as relaxation when it's done with—or for—someone you love. Why find meaning in the routine tasks we do each day? Because most of our day is spent with routine work and school and housekeeping. If we wait until relaxing times to enjoy life we'd waste away most of our lives. Besides, garages have to be cleaned, homework has to be done, and bills must be paid. So why not add heart to them? Why not work for satisfaction in a job well done no matter how distasteful the task? The Bible explains: "Whatever you do, work at it with all your heart, as working for the Lord, not for men" (Colossians 3:23).

Small children understand this. They turn inside out with excitement when it comes time to help Dad do the dishes or Mom paint the bedroom. They want to be significant. They want to make a difference. They understand that being together adds cheer to the chore. Preserve this pride in honest hard work with your own enthusiasm and motivation.

"Who wants to clean out the garage with me on Saturday?" offered Jared.

"I will!" enthused Greg.

"Can I help, too?" asked Gina.

"Remember? Last time we found our old roller skates that had been missing for weeks!" said Ben.

"Yeah, it will be like a treasure hunt," said Gina.

Greg, Gina, and Ben didn't continue the same enthusiasm after an hour of work in a cluttered garage. But a little inventiveness gave them the oomph they needed to finish the job. It went like this on that Saturday:

"How long are we going to have to work?" asked Greg, wanting to be with Dad but getting a little tired of all the effort.

"It will take most of the morning, but we'll make it fun," said Jared.

"Well, I'm getting tired," said Greg. "I've changed my mind about wanting to help."

"We're all getting tired," Jared countered. "But I need you to stay with us. The garage has got to be cleaned, so let's do it together."

"Why don't you and Mom just do it?" suggested Greg.

"Because Mom and I are only two people, and because Mom is working on another cleaning project inside," explained Jared. "Besides, we're not the only two who use this garage."

"But we don't want to do it," said Gina. "Can't we quit and do it again another day?"

"Another day tends not to come. Today is the day," insisted Jared. "Now let's work for thirty more minutes and then we'll take a cookie break."

"Can I bring music out?" asked Greg.

"That would be a good idea. But be back with your CD player in 90 seconds," said Jared, conscious of how tempting it would be to take a long time getting the music.

After the break they worked well for about nine minutes.

"Can I quit now?" asked Gina.

> No matter whether the day is a holiday or routine, cultivate the habit of looking forward to, and treasuring, each new day.

"No, we've got a ways to go," said Jared. "Now that we've got the biggest part done, let's divide the garage into sections and each of you can be responsible for your own part. You can make your section beautiful, and we'll all admire it!"

"Will there be prizes for the best section?" Ben interjected, suddenly interested.

"Maybe not competitive prizes, but there's definitely ice cream waiting when each of you finishes your section," said Jared. "I think Mama bought several kinds of syrups and toppings."

"I'll go ask," volunteered Greg.

"No thanks," said Jared. "I know we'll be having ice cream at noon. Let's keep at this until the top of the hour and then we'll all take a break and go look."

Through both work time and playtime, build a river of family joy so strong that sadness can't budge it. Because this joy will be based in Jesus Christ, your family will have the underlying power to make it through the roughest of storms. Sadness will interrupt happiness, but you can walk through the sorrowful times without fear.

You can feel your sadness, talk about it, understand it, and then act upon it to move past the sad back to happy again.

JOY TIP

Every day is a unique creation deserving celebration. It won't always be with cake and ice cream but it can always include an element of anticipation, a tidbit of togetherness, an ingredient of sharing, and a component of memory making.

7

HER FEVER JUST KEEPS GOING UP

Because of the Lord's great love we are not consumed, for his compassions never fail. They are new every morning; great is your faithfulness.

—Lamentations 3:22–23

"I can't see, Mom. Something's wrong with my eyes. There are big black spots wherever I look, and I can't see," said Sarah with confusion.

"What do you mean you can't see?" I forced a calm voice to ask. "Did you look out the window and then back in? Sometimes the brightness of the outside makes the inside seem dark."

"It's not just dark; I can't see anything out of certain parts of my eyes," said Sarah. "How can I pack?" With the lovely perspective of a child, Sarah worried more about the trip we were packing for than her failing vision.

"I'll take your job for a while. Why don't you try lying down with your eyes closed for just a minute?" I suggested with more composure than I felt.

No vision? What did this mean? Was she losing her sight? Could an illness do this temporarily? What should I do? I wondered if I could get her into an eye doctor that afternoon. Or was a neurologist the doctor for this problem? My mind recoiled from the thought that maybe a tumor was pressing on her optic nerve—I'd heard of that. While she rested I'd try to figure out what to do. I asked God to guide me. Just then she started to vomit.

I leapt for the trash can to catch whatever hadn't already spewed.

She finished and said, "My head, oh my head!"

After I helped Sarah out of her messy clothes and into clean ones she laid back on the bed in misery. "My head! My head! It hurts so much! Close the curtains. Please!"

That's it! I realized, recalling my splitting headache from two days before. *Maybe Sarah was getting what I had.* Because it was unusual for me to waken with a headache, I had attributed it to some sort of virus. That horrible headache was accompanied by room-spinning nausea. As long as I lay perfectly still, I was fine. Sitting or walking was out of the question. I was the kind of person who went to work even with the flu, but whatever this was, it forced me to sleep or stay perfectly still all day.

That must be what's wrong with her, I thought with relief and sympathy.

I knew firsthand how horrible she felt. If I hadn't just had it, I'd have been really worried. But because I'd gotten better, I knew she would. She wasn't going blind or facing an optic nerve tumor. She'd simply caught the virus I had. My headache and nausea hadn't lasted over a day, so I felt it safe to assure her.

"You should feel much better in a few hours. It looks like you caught the virus I had."

"Okay," she said weakly. Though not enthusiastic that I'd shared my germ with her, she did seem somewhat relieved that there might be an end in sight.

"Can you see any better?" I asked, wondering if the sight problems were related to this virus.

"I don't know. My eyes are closed," she answered, as though that were so logical I should have recognized it.

Oh, the humor of the ill. Rather than push her to open her eyes, I decided it might be safe to wait a few minutes. I left to rinse out the trash can and get wet rags to clean the carpet.

Why do we always have grape juice before vomiting hits? I lamented as I re-entered the room. I looked past the half-packed suitcase to Sarah. She had fallen sound asleep.

I quietly finished the clean-up and pitched Sarah's clothes into the washing machine. I raised a prayer of thanks for indoor plumbing and a working washing machine. Just then I heard the sounds of vomiting again. I raced to Sarah, grateful to find her holding the trash can. I held it for her and stroked her head.

"Will we get to go tomorrow?" Sarah asked. Emily poked her head in the door to hear the answer.

"I don't know, honey. We'll just have to wait and see," I said honestly, motioning Emily out of the room. I wished I knew the answer.

All that day Sarah woke, vomited, and then fell asleep again. All that day we wondered if we'd get to go on our long-awaited trip. Illness comes at the least convenient times. And quite honestly, I can't think of any time that is convenient for illness.

How do we enjoy the illness and injury part of life with our children?

We don't.

Cancer, vomiting, accidents, and infections aren't meant to be enjoyed. They're miserable insults to our good God. Illness-causing bacteria are distortions of the good bacteria that normally help our stomachs and other body organs function well. Viruses are invaders that have no right to call our bodies home. Cancer is distorted cells that won't do their usual functions. It's okay to call illness bad. It's okay to cry when you're hurt. We must love the things God loves and hate the things God hates. Part of true enjoyment is knowing what to fret over.

So why a chapter on illness in a book about growing a family that enjoys life together? Because how we handle our fretting is as important as how we handle our joys. Will we approach the grief of illness honestly and directly, or will we whine and demand special treatment? Will we display self-pity or selflessly move past our aching hearts to show kindness? Will we rally as a family to attack the problem, or will we bite at each other?

Choose Patience and Peace

No one likes to clean up vomit. No one likes to change an entire bed with all four layers splattered by a nosebleed. No one feels like getting up at midnight when the alarm goes off to dispense the next dose of medicine. We do it and we do it patiently because a person needs our help. Patience isn't something we feel or don't feel. It's something we choose to use. Those amazing parents who display constant patience with their kids aren't super-heroes. They're regular human beings who decide to show care for people who matter— their children. Patience starts with your head; decide to care, even when you feel like biting. Look past your own anguish to see the hurting person in front of you. Then watch your heart follow.

You and your sick child aren't the only ones who need patience. Your well children need you too. When Sarah was sick that packing day, Emily and I were both worried and consequently short-tempered. I kept wanting to correct Emily. She kept wanting me to back off. Every time Sarah woke and vomited I had to leave Emily with the work. And though I thought Sarah had the same virus I'd had earlier, nagging fears tormented me. Was this vomiting a sign of a neurological problem? Did she have a blockage? Were the vision problems signs of a fatal condition?

"Emily, I know I'm irritable," I finally said.

"That's for sure," she said with both seriousness and teasing.

"I think it's because I'm worried about Sarah and wish she wasn't sick," I suggested. "Plus we both have extra work. Let's tread lightly around each other."

> Cancer, catastrophe, car accidents, and the like aren't meant to be enjoyed. Part of true enjoyment is knowing what to fret over. Love the things God loves, and hate the things God hates.

On top of all our other worries, we had to wait. We wouldn't know for several hours if Sarah's symptoms were serious enough to warrant postponing our trip. I didn't like waiting. I wanted to know now. Worse, we might not know even after waiting.

"Mom, why does someone in our family always get sick on the big days?" asked Emily

"I don't know, honey, but it sure seems that way," I agreed. "Germs are everywhere and all families get them sometimes. I wish we hadn't gotten this one."

When our children ask why, they don't want a big explanation as much as they want the illness to stop. We must recognize illness as the goodness-stealer it is and treat it as such. Illness isn't a punishment or a blessing. It's a fact of life in our imperfect world (Matthew 5:45). And it's not a fun fact.

"What if I get it next?" she asked. "I don't want to be sick like that while we're gone."

"And I don't want you to," I answered. "I think Sarah has what I had on the weekend. And your stomach hurt really badly last night. You never vomited but I think you had a touch of it then. So I think you've already had it." We parents are frequently called on to diagnose and treat illnesses before we contact a doctor. We have to notice how the illness acts and how it might spread to other family members. We decide if we need a doctor, when we need a doctor, and what to say when we call. We must recognize when the illness is really over, and when we must stay home. None of that is easy.

"Good," she said with obvious relief. "And the vomiting only lasts a day so we can go tomorrow, right?"

"I hope so," I responded. "I hate sickness, don't you?"

"Yes," agreed Emily.

Illness, quite simply, is a thief. It steals time, togetherness, and energy. Sarah would much rather have shared the agony and ecstasy of packing, the anticipation and preparation for our trip. She had wanted to mix the travel snacks and pack a surprise travel bag for Emily. She had planned to attend the school play that evening. But illness stole all of these. Illness also steals time with friends and family. What if this illness preempted our long-awaited visit with our friend from Ecuador? She would only be in the states for a few days—we'd miss her totally if this illness persisted. Even so, we couldn't use that as an excuse to go while Sarah was ill. It would be heartless to share this miserable illness and let her take it home to her family and neighbors.

Resist the holy-sounding-but-simply-not-true "This is a blessing in disguise." Go ahead and call illness bad. Refuse to repeat "God gives us only what we can handle." It's a misquote of 1 Corinthians 10:13, a verse on temptation, not illness. Your kids know many ornery people who have very little illness; and they know very good people who have died of disease. Germs are not doled out by faith; they're part of that groaning creation described in Romans 8:22. God is the giver of good gifts, not of stones and snakes (Matthew 7:9–12; 1 John 1:5).

Refuse to blame God for the suffering of this world. Instead, let Him help you work around it. Find His ways to care for your sick family member as well as those who are still healthy.

A Silly Mother's Guide to Infection Prevention

Life is too short to spend unnecessary time sick. There's no way to prevent all infections, but we can prevent many of them:

Elbow Elevators: Most infections are transmitted by touch. So push elevator buttons with your elbows to keep touch-borne germs from getting on your hands and into your body.

Hip Doors: Push doors open with your back or hip to avoid picking up germs. Or grab vertical handles on the bottom rather than the more frequently touched tops.

Wash Hands. Even unsilly researchers agree that this is the single-most effective disease prevention. Wash your hands to keep germs you touch from entering your eyes, mouth, and nose. Wash before meals, after coming home, and when the house is full of company.

Personal Towels: Especially when someone in your house is sick, minimize germ transfer with personal towels or frequent towel changing. Even the most careful hand washers rub some contagion onto their towels. Paper or personal cups work toward the same purpose.

Honesty: When one of you has had the flu, tell friends and relatives before they come to your home or you go to theirs. Then they can decide if they want to take the risk. Even if the illness is over for one, another family member may be getting it. Inconvenience yourself rather than sentence a friend or relative to suffer through the misery you just endured.

Work Together

By late afternoon Sarah began to perk up. The vomiting stopped and she sat up to sip root beer. This brought a new set of struggles.

"Tell Emily to quit bragging about going to the play!" Sarah complained.

"She's not bragging, she's excited," I clarified.

Then I privately warned Emily, "Sarah feels rotten so please keep your exuberance down. I know you're excited, and so you should be. But be considerate, please. She wants to go."

"If you had any heart at all, you wouldn't talk about that play so much," said Sarah piteously.

"I can't help it if you're sick and I'm not," Emily defended herself.

"Sarah, you can't use your illness as an excuse to gripe at Emily," I mediated. "And, Emily, you can't help Sarah's illness, but you can help how you treat her."

"But I don't feel good, and she does," said Sarah.

"True. But feeling good or feeling rotten, you've got to be kind," I insisted.

"But I don't think it's fair that I always have to give in to her," said Emily.

"That's not what I'm asking," I said. "You're right. It wouldn't be fair to always give in. What I'm asking is that you consider her feelings. Maybe talk a little less about the play, refill her glass, do something nice. Treat her like you'd want to be treated if you were sick and missing the play."

"What if I bring you a program and tell you about the play?" offered Emily, as a branch of peace.

"Will you get me some autographs too?" added Sarah.

"I'll try," said Emily. "Sometimes the actors don't come out."

"Thanks, Emily," I said. "And thanks, Sarah, for taking the whine out of your voice."

Humoring the patient sounds nice, but it's dangerous. It leads to moaning and self-pity that make the whole family miserable. It feeds a sick image, the feeling your child can't do things on her own or that others owe her help. Even worse, the sick one may enjoy the attention so much that she assumes being sick is the way to keep it. Prevent all of this by giving attention for other-centeredness rather than self-pity.

We've learned the hard way that kindness is better than catering, sensitivity is better than sick-focus, mutuality is better than me-me-me. No matter how ill, the sick one can be nice. She won't have the same level of energy or patience, but she can still choose to show care. When Sarah sees the ear doctor she sometimes brings Emily the prize she gets at the end. When Emily spent Christmas morning in the emergency room with a high fever, she brought Sarah an extra tongue depressor. These acts of kindness help not only the well one, but the sick one. Sarah forgets about her ear troubles when she's picking a prize for Emily. While she's hiding Sarah's tongue depressor behind her back, Emily forgets that she had to have a blood test rather than play longer with her new Christmas gifts. And Bill and I smile to see our daughters be good to each other. All of us see God's Word in action: when we love others as we love ourselves, good comes to every family member (Mark 12:31).

> The way we handle our fretting is as important as the way we handle our happiness. Will we rally as a family to attack a problem, or will we bite at each other?

Know Illness

We make our children's illnesses more bearable and safe as we calmly do what we know to do—or at least try. To grow this calmness, learn about illness. How does it work? What kinds of illnesses are there? Which ones are contagious and how do you treat each? My identifying what might have been wrong with Sarah came from years of doctor visits, pages of writing down doctor's instructions, repeated references to parents' medical guides, and careful learning from other parents. Our knowledge as parents can't replace doctors, but it equips us to work hand in hand with them to find the best diagnosis and treatment. Following is Dr. Mom's summary of what makes our children sick.

The three basic illness-causers are viruses, bacteria, and allergies.

- *Viruses* are microscopic organisms with great variety and a mean impact. They infect the body with such miseries as the stomach flu and chicken pox, colds and winter achy flu, severe sore throats and croup, rashes and stomachaches. Viruses tend to give a low-grade fever, though some viral fevers are quite high. Viruses last one to five days, and are not cured by any medicine. Only time, symptom relief, and love can help us through most of them. A few viruses, such as polio and chicken pox, now have vaccines to prevent them. Even then, we "catch" a bit of the illness and our body fights it off. Viruses appear to be responsible for most illnesses. Viruses are highly contagious.

- *Bacteria* are larger than viruses, and cause big illnesses. Viruses tend to impact the body widely; bacteria prefer to concentrate in one area like the throat, ear, or urinary tract. Fevers with bacteria tend to go higher than viral fevers, but not always. Bacteria cause strep throat, some ear infections, bladder and kidney infections, and whole-body illnesses that plague children. Bacterial infections are usually contagious. Antibiotics will fight them, but resist the urge to use leftover antibiotics. Why? (1) There shouldn't be any if you took your last prescription properly. (2) You must take antibiotics for a full course to kill the infection; giving only a dose or two may strengthen the infection rather than eliminate it. (3) Each antibiotic impacts only certain bacteria, so you must match the right antibiotic to the infection. Interestingly, helpful bacteria are everywhere: on your skin, in the air, in the soil, and more. No one quite knows why some become harmful.

> There are:
> Three basic illness-causers,
> Two ways to treat illnesses,
> One good illness fighter, which sometimes needs help.

- *Allergies* are not infections at all, but the body's confusion over the danger of its environment. Allergies happen when your body reacts to common substances like dust, pollen, and animal dander. If you're allergic to these, you sneeze, wheeze, break out in hives, develop a rash, or worse. Bee stings and penicillin can cause anaphylactic allergies in sensitive persons—a reaction that can kill. Thankfully these are rare. Is your child allergic? Don't believe a doctor who just examines and declares allergy. Only allergy tests can tell. If your child does have allergies, he may outgrow them or may be desensitized with a series of allergy shots. Allergies respond to medicine only symptomatically—medications can stop the signs of allergy, even stop a fatal reaction, but can't cure it. This relief matters, but don't confuse it with cure.

This leads us to the two basic illness treatments: cures and symptom-relievers.

A *cure* stops the infection; symptom relief just makes it look and feel as though the illness is gone. Aspirin, acetaminophen, antihistamines, and decongestants are common symptom relievers. They make you feel better, but the infection still lurks and is still contagious. Antibiotics cure strep throats. Chemotherapy can cure cancer. But there's no cure for the common cold or the flu. We can only do what makes us feel better until our body heals. Decongestants and pain relievers are real medicine; but again, they don't *cure* the illness. As my grandfather used to say, "A cold will go away in six days with medicine, half-a-dozen without it." For bacterial illnesses your doctor may prescribe cure combined with symptom relief: When your child gets a painful ear infection, for example, you may receive two prescriptions—an antibiotic to cure the infection and an ear drop to ease the pain until then. The drop numbs the ear so your child feels better immediately. But his ear still needs the antibiotic to heal. One caution with symptomatic relief: an illness needing antibiotics help may grow worse while masked by symptom relievers. Check with your doctor to get the treatment you need.

No matter what ails your body, you have a strong ally. This one strong fighter is the body itself.

With viruses and many bacterial infections, your child's body will get rid of the offending organism all by itself. It sends white blood cells and raises body temperature to stop the germs. Some doctors recommend not reducing tolerable fevers, which allows the fever to "cook" the illness. To fight stronger bacteria and to cope with certain allergies, your body needs help. Doctor-prescribed antibiotics work with your body to cure the illnesses. Allergy shots help your body learn a friendly response to pollen, dust, and animal dander. Emergency injections can block fatal allergic reactions.

This chart puts Dr. Mom's advice in a nutshell:

	VIRUS	BACTERIA	ALLERGY
FEVER	Often	Often	No
HELPED BY MEDICINE	No	Yes	Symptomatically
CONTAGIOUS	Yes	Yes	No
WHEN TO GO OUT	24 hours of no fever and no fever reducer	24 hours of no fever and 24 hours on medication	When not around allergen

Decide What to Do

What was wrong with Sarah? The vision problem went away when the vomiting started, so that would rule out tumors or worse. There was no fever, so it was unlikely to be a bacterial infection. Headache and vomiting come with many viruses, so maybe it was a virus. But was I right? Could vision problems come and go? Was the vomiting a sign of something much worse than the stomach flu? I asked God to give me a sense of what to do. I decided to wait and watch.

Watchful waiting works well in most circumstances. If we're wrong, the severity of symptoms will let us know. *Fridays* and *mamahunches* are two exceptions to the watchful waiting rule. If it's Friday at 4:00 P.M. and Sarah, who's super-prone to ear infections, mentions one word about her ears being painful we head straight to the doctor. Her own pediatrician knows her thickened-by-infection eardrums well and is better able to diagnose her than an on-call physician who doesn't know her medical history.

Emily once had a fever of 104 and her throat hurt so badly she could hardly talk. Every muscle in her body ached. I was certain she had the worst case of strep throat ever. It was Saturday—of course—and our family doctor wasn't on hand. But I had a hunch we couldn't wait until Monday. I took her to a weekend clinic, where they ran a throat culture and blood work. They verified that it wasn't strep but a virus, probably an early case of the flu. *The flu! In August?* I was incredulous. Then I remembered the body aches. My mama-hunch had been wrong; but even so, it was good to know for sure. She was so sick for the rest of the weekend that I would have been certain she was dying had she not been diagnosed.

When Sarah's symptoms repeated themselves four months later, I learned from her doctor that Sarah's illness may not have been a virus at all, but a migraine headache. The vision loss, followed by headache, followed by vomiting and ultra-sensitivity to any sensory information were classic migraine symptoms. Migraines are exceptions to the three basic-illness-causers rule. So are cancer, rheumatoid arthritis, asthma, cystic fibrosis, heart disease, and more.

We once missed our Granddaddy's birthday party because Emily had a high fever that wouldn't quit. We didn't want Granddad to catch whatever virus or bacteria was causing it. But the illness turned out to be cancer—not at all contagious, but the start of two painful years of chemotherapy and praying. That's five years behind us now, thankfully, and we're back to dealing with viruses. But really severe illnesses can and do happen.

Should I worry about cancer when my child's fever won't go down? Should I worry about asthma each time she wheezes? Is the rash a signal of an arthritis flare-up? Maybe. But I start with the simple three: virus, bacteria, and allergy. Then I watch. A cancer fever stays for weeks. An arthritis flare-up has other distinct characteristics. Cystic fibrosis has genetic components. Migraines have no fever. And so on. It's complicated and frightening to figure out what's going on in a listless child's body. But I write and date exactly what I see, mentally noting what I don't have time to write. If I'm not sure, I talk over her symptoms with her doctors.

Why all this talk about illness? Because the better you understand it, the more calmly you can help your child. My book *When a Hug Won't Fix the Hurt: Walking With Your Child Through Crisis* offers actions to help your family walk through life-threatening illnesses, disabilities, and other painful times. It also offers specific ways friends can help.

Team Up With a Good Doctor

God gave you and your children bodies that in most cases take good care of themselves. But sometimes you need antibiotics or other medicine. Doctors can help even when you don't need medicine by discerning what's wrong so you know what to do to help heal it. When you and your child visit the doctor, though, know that we're a long way from the Star Trek technology where we can scan the body and know just what's going on. No doctor, no matter how skilled, can tell the difference between a virus, a bacteria, or an allergy simply through an examination. Without running cultures, no doctor knows exactly what antibiotic will treat your child's bacterial infection. So what do you do? You work with a doctor to solve a mystery.

When I take my child to the doctor, he gathers several clues. He talks with my child and then me to understand the symptoms and history of the illness. Has anyone else had similar symptoms, and what were the results? He examines my child to find more clues. Depending on what he finds, he might order a blood test to indicate whether the germ is a virus or a bacteria. Or he might choose a throat culture to distinguish strep throat, which needs medicine, from viral throat infections, which won't respond to medicine. A urine culture tells him whether my child's sore back is caused by a urinary tract infection or not. Allergy tests indicate whether she tends toward allergies. A different blood test would rule out cancer and other serious illnesses. Because medicine advances rapidly, he'll likely have even more strategies to gather clues by the time this book is published. And taking all these clues together we decide the best way to treat the illness.

When your God-given hunch indicates your child needs to see a doctor, pick a good one. Some very nice doctors work from their pet ideas rather than sound medical practice. Others pronounce illness as allergy, asthma, or strep without the necessary tests. They might miss an illness needing more than symptomatic treatment. They might over-treat with antibiotic when unnecessary. Other doctors are so cautious that they routinely order a multiplicity of expensive tests. Avoid doctors who claim easy answers, rush through visits, refuse to listen to your hunches, or treat your child harshly. Instead, pick a doctor who is perceptive, thorough without being alarmist, and attentive to your child. Choose one who takes time to educate you, who employs caring nurses, and who treats your family as valuable members of the health-care team. Doctors are not a step above you, nor do they know everything. They're people who happen to have studied medicine and practice applying it to real children. Together, the two of you treat your child.

There's a third person on the healing team, and the primary member—God himself. God has given us an immune system able to independently fight off most illnesses. And He has guided bright minds to find medicines and treatments to help those illnesses that our immune system can't handle alone. Through all this He promises to guide us.

> "Is any one of you sick? He should call the elders of the church to pray over him and anoint him with oil in the name of the Lord. . . . Pray for each other so you may be healed. The prayer of a righteous man is powerful and effective" (James 5:14, 16).

It's not that the righteous elders pray better; it's that the sick one might be too ill to pray for himself. The anointing oil symbolizes the touch of God on the sick one's life. God always does the healing, whether through your body's immune system or with a little help from medicine and treatments with which He has provided us.

Be True Even When It's Hard

When Sarah got sick, I had to be honest about the reality of the illness. I couldn't just wish it away or dose it with acetaminophen and pretend she was better. I once came down with a stomach virus while visiting relatives for Thanksgiving. By that Sunday ten family members were miserably suffering from the virus I shared. I felt simply terrible that I had caused such torment. I couldn't help it then because I didn't know I was getting sick. But I could help it this time because Sarah was already sick.

It's definitely harder on me to do the loving thing—to keep my child home so the illness won't spread to others. But it's worth it for the sake of the people I love. To create joy, not squash it, wait to be around other people until you or your child is twenty-four hours fever-free. Because most fevers go down in the morning and up in the evening, don't assume a normal morning temperature means the illness is over. And because pain relievers artificially reduce a fever, make sure the span of time with no fever happens with no aspirin or acetaminophen in your child's system.

Living in a family complicates things even further. As one child recovers from an illness, the others may be coming down with it. An illness is most contagious the day before or the day you actually become ill. So watch *all* family members for recovery before gathering with friends and family.

It's hard to be true. But knowing the truth can help. Spot the falsehoods in each of these statements:

MYTH: *If it doesn't respond to antibiotics, it's an allergy and I don't have to worry about it being contagious. I can go ahead and take him to his friend's house or to church.* It could be an allergy. But it's more likely a virus. Viruses are very contagious, can make friends severely ill. Keep your child away from other children until fever and symptoms are gone. Only time and rest heal them.

MYTH: *Teething causes fever.* How would a natural bodily process like tooth eruption cause illness, runny nose, and fever? Illness, runny nose, and fever are caused by germs, not teeth. The reason teething gets blamed is that you can almost always find a tooth erupting in a baby's mouth. And babies get an average of twelve illnesses a year. If your child has a fever or other symptoms of illness, he or she needs treatment.

MYTH: *Acetaminophen and aspirin cure fevers.* Fever is not an illness; it's a symptom of an illness. Pain relievers reduce the fever, but the illness must be cured by antibiotics or by your body's immune system.

Make It Through the Tunnel

Some illnesses last a single day. Most last two to five days. And then some last up to a lifetime.

What do you do with those seemingly endless hours that pile up while waiting for a fever to break or for the illness to end? Think of it as a tunnel—a time of going through the darkness when you can't always see the end. Then turn the lights on in that tunnel with interesting activities, being in the same room, conversations, routines, and assurances that better days are coming. For year-long illnesses and non-contagious illnesses, continue school, church, and other routines as much as physically possible. This normalcy distracts from the pain of the illness, and keeps it from controlling your child's life.

Relief during Illness

These simple tools can take the edge off the physical and emotional strain of illness:

Silly straws: Your child needs fluids but has no desire to drink. Help out with crazy drinking cups and looping straws. We once found a straw shaped like a pair of glasses. You put one end in your drink and the other around your face and into your mouth—the liquid goes from the glass, over an ear, around both eyes, over the other ear, and into your waiting mouth. Lots of fun, and the liquid cools fevered brows.

Sleeping bags: Ill children want to be near their parents. Lay your sick child's sleeping bag next to wherever you'll be most of the day. Then move him when you move. The sleeping bag feels less isolating than a bed and it keeps them warm.

Picture books, puzzles, and pops: You never know when the flu will invade your house, and when it comes you'll have little energy or freedom to get supplies. So keep frozen fruit bars, a variety of picture and new puzzle books handy. Flavored ices taste good when nothing else does. Offer books when your child says, "I want to do something but I don't feel strong enough to get up." Even teenagers like their childhood picture books when they feel horrible.

Compete with the audience: Let illness be the one time you let your children watch daytime television. Rather than be bored by talk shows and insulted by soap operas, challenge your children to win game shows.

I'm the star: Pull out home videos and tell stories about your child when she was younger. There is nothing more entertaining than watching yourself on video, unless it's watching your parents as children. Your kids want to know what you did, felt, said, and thought as a child. They want to know the same things about themselves.

Relief During Illness (continued)

Story tapes: Invite a grandparent to tell stories on tape. Play these to give the fun of a story with the comfort of Grandmama's voice. It's almost as good as having her there. Prerecorded story tapes serve a similar purpose. Many public libraries carry these.

Flip books and rebuses: Your pre-readers will especially like these. Rebuses are pictures in the place of words. Flip books make the picture "move" when you flip the pages. Older children will enjoy drawing their own flip books with a small spiral notebook.

Markers in all varieties: Smelly markers, markers that change colors, markers with fancy tips, wide and thin markers, and many more are available to make drawing fun. Colored pencils help too.

Your presence: Especially when your children don't feel like doing any of the above, they want you. Hold them when their fever makes them feel miserable. Rock them as they try to get to sleep. Hold back their hair, cool their brow with a wet cloth when they are vomiting. Sit nearby while they sleep. Even a gangly eighteen-year-old wants attention when he feels rotten.

EMLA® cream: If your child must have a shot or other needle procedure, ask your doctor about this prescription medicine that numbs skin so well that children can't feel the needle. It must be applied an hour ahead of time.

Help: Once your child is better, listen for other families who might have illness. Because you know how cooped up and powerless illness makes you feel, offer to run errands for friends whose children are sick. Go by the library for new books or bring a special food from the grocery. You'll bring joy to both your friends and your own family.

As Sarah became more perky, I asked her, "Do you feel like a puzzle book?"

"No, I feel too weak," Sarah answered. "I want something to do, but nothing I have to think about."

"Why don't you get your headphones and try listening to story tapes," I suggested. Sarah shrugged.

"Will I ever feel good again?" Sarah worried.

"Certainly," I assured her. "Most of these vomiting viruses last one or two days. You're almost finished with day one, so you should start feeling better soon."

"But it seems like it's already been forever!" she lamented.

"Time seems longer because you've been so miserable," I explained. "A day of Christmas just zips by. This rough day is almost over."

We seek answers and apply tender loving care while we walk through agonizing days with our children. Perhaps the most comforting truth of all is that God goes with us. Even though you and your children "walk through the valley of the shadow of death" you can "fear no evil" because God is with you (Psalm 23:4).

Perhaps fear is the very emotion that makes it so hard for us to be calm and caring during illness. We fear the illness will permanently hurt our children; we fear the others will get it; we fear that it is life-threatening. These fears make sense. Talk with God about them and then deliberately turn your eyes upon Jesus. Let Him give you peace in the midst of anguish. Notice that He's right there walking with you through this dangerous time.

Celebrate When Health Comes

Amazingly, Sarah was better by evening. She felt as good that night as she had felt bad that morning. We kept her home from the play, though she begged to go. Because most illnesses worsen at night, evening wellness was a reliable indicator of health. But we needed to watch to be certain how she felt was true recovery rather than a momentary burst of energy.

With no more sign of illness the next day, we left for the trip. Our hearts were especially grateful. No one else got the illness, and Sarah remained energetic and bubbly during our entire visit. We were so thankful that we felt like celebrating.

So we did.

Why did Sarah get well in one day when illnesses in our house typically last three or more days? That's simply the way it worked. Recovery from illness is not a sign of God's favor any more than failure to recover means He's angry with you. Illness is a part of this sin-tainted world we live in. Pain is an equal-opportunity joy-stealer. And we attack it as such.

Whether the illness is day-long or lifelong, we can make it through because of certain hope: Jesus will return and personally wipe away our tears. There will be no more crying or pain. Whether on earth or in heaven, the pain will stop. "He will wipe away every tear from their eyes. There will be no more death or mourning or crying or pain, for the old order of things has passed away" (Revelation 21:4).

Joy Tip

Not all of life is a picnic. We can't enjoy illness in the giddy sense of the word. But we can make the pain more bearable by going though the dark days as a team. Rally as a family to attack the illness, tenderly care for each other, and move toward the light.

8

JUST WAIT TILL THEY BECOME TEENAGERS!

"For I know the plans I have for you," declares the LORD, "plans to prosper you and not to harm you, plans to give you hope and a future."

—Jeremiah 29:11

"Just wait until your children become teenagers," my well-meaning friend warned. "All the fun turns to agony and you lose the closeness you have with your children."

I've been a little nervous about that.

Did I start to lose closeness when my happy kindergartner Emily bounced into the school without a glance back? Or when she returned full of stories about the day rather than crying because she missed me?

Did the distance begin when fifth-grade Sarah went on a field trip by herself, adding up the prices of fast-food entrees ahead of time so she'd be certain to have enough food money left after the gift shop? Did it happen when she not only found out the food amounts but added up two choices, and then attached a sticky note to her dollar bills to remind her how much to save depending on how hungry she felt?

Or did we lose closeness when Emily surreptitiously warned Sarah, "You just gotta get used to it. Mom likes to be involved. Just explain when you need to do it yourself."

Could it be happening now that I can no longer say, "I love you" in public, or now that my teenagers walk several paces behind me with specific instructions to pretend I don't know them if a peer comes along?

Absolutely not.

We're not losing. We're gaining. We're gaining joy. At one and the same time I'm learning my limits and delighting that my daughters are persistently taking responsibility for making their own place at school and in the world. And while I won't be there to make sure my Sarah has enough money, she'll experience the pride of managing her finances on her own. When I recognize that walking separately from my girls gives people opportunity to see and know them as unique people, not extensions of me, I'm glad to tease rather than lament about being an embarrassing mother.

I'm learning not to put much stake in prophecies of doom. Instead I'm listening to wise friends who tell of adult closeness with their parents, a closeness that grew rocky for a while but never collapsed. Certainly my teenage daughters have adolescent attacks, those moments when their emotions rage out of control and everything is either wonderful or terrible. Certainly I have days when I'm the most unreasonable mother ever born. But more frequent are the new and interesting ways to relate to increasingly mature and insightful people—my daughters.

What makes the difference between a happy and a miserable adolescence?

Letting go.

A family that enjoys each other balances closeness with independence, a cozy experience in the nest with encouragement to take wing.

Begin the Tapestry

When my girls were small they liked to weave paper place mats. At first Bill or I would cut the paper strips and the paper warp to weave them in. It didn't take long for the girls to do their own cutting, happily making zigzags and ocean waves as well as checkerboards. They graduated to potholders and then an intriguing five-finger weaving that made long belts and fancy scarves. Sarah is now a detailed wool weaver, adding hand-stitched designs to her loom-generated creations. The girls' weavings become beautiful with the materials they choose and the dedication they put into them. From simple weavings to intricate ones, they have found joy in the process and pride in lovely finished products.

Letting our children go is similar. Neither is easy, but both produce beautiful results. Many were the times Sarah got tired and didn't want to finish a weaving she'd begun. She much preferred starting something new to finishing a project in process. But I would prod her to finish one project before she

> When our children grow up, we're not losing joy. We're gaining.

began another. The exciting effect was a pillow, purse, or place mat she would give with pleasure. Now she provides her own motivation to finish, keeping the next project as a reward for finishing the first. And she finds joy in the doing.

When third-grader Emily first attended summer camp, my heart wanted to keep her home safe and sound. But at the same time I wanted for her the adventure of sleeping outdoors, of making crafts, of falling in the creek. So we talked about some of the things she'd experience: "When you're at camp you may get a tight feeling in your stomach and wish you were home. That's called homesickness. It usually comes at night when you're lying in your bed. If it happens, think about all the happy things you did during the day and what you'll do again the next morning. Talk with God to let Him know you're glad you have a home to miss. Then ask Him to comfort you and move your thoughts to the fun of camp.

"The good thing about camp is that homesickness isn't the only thing you'll feel. You'll feel excitement when you find your first salamander, or hop rocks across a creek without falling in. You'll feel cozy when you sing around the campfire at night, or lie on the grass, looking at the stars. You'll feel friendship when you and your cabin mates scale the obstacle course wall. You'll feel pride when you make something fun in the craft shop. Won't camp be great!"

Emily was more than excited about the salamanders, obstacle course, campfires, and friendships. She didn't give much thought to homesickness. But she experienced it. Upon returning home she reported, "A lot of the kids cried at night, but I knew what that sad feeling was and what to do about it. I tried to think about all the happy things that had happened that day, but it made me want to tell you about them and the homesickness got worse. So I just did the talking to God part. Just about the time I'd get really lonely, I'd fall asleep. Then in the morning I was much too busy to get homesick."

For a moment I felt a little sad that she didn't have more trouble being away. But I was equally proud that she didn't. Parenting is a delightful adventure of working ourselves out of a job. Enjoying each other means we move our children—or let them move—to the point where they don't need us every minute of every day. The delight doesn't always come in the process. But it does come as we see the pattern take shape, and ultimately in the final product. Like Sarah I'd often rather quit than keep going. I prefer to keep my girls close by, rather than finish this parenting job. But when I watch them triumph at camp, or in money management, or in people skills, the exhilaration is worth all the struggle. As I grant my children independent identities, they bring their friends home comfortably, and we continue to share life. We grow closer than ever.

> **Backing off doesn't mean we back away. We absolutely must continue to express affection, guidance, and interest. But we change the designs.**

Children have a natural drive toward independence. Together with God we must let them live that freedom and live it with success. As we let them go in age-appropriate ways and show them how to handle what they face, they will soar. And we'll have the pleasure of watching them fly.

See the Colors You Have to Work With

One of the greatest pleasures of children who are growing in independence is their ability to give joy to others—both in and out of the family—rather than be receivers only.

This pleasure doesn't start at age thirteen or eighteen. It grows from birth. My sister-in-law recently showed me a photo of my two-year-old Sarah taken years before. She was so cherubic and happy, toddling with eagerness toward her cousins. The picture made us

133

CHRISTIANS REALLY DO HAVE MORE FUN

Many teens think fast driving, loads of liquor, lots of boy-friends and girlfriends, and daring stunts are the keys to adulthood. Refuse to let these steal the real fun. Here are ways you can teach your teen to have a better kind of fun:

I-make-the-fun attitude: Impart to your children the certainty that they can make their own fun. They don't have to wait for money or transportation or entertainment. They can gather one or more friends, add an idea and conversation, and have the time of their lives. If friends are busy, they can create solo fun with a good book, a hobby, or a pursuit. This is the opposite of "There's nothing to do in this town."

Adult entrees: When your preteen outgrows the kiddie menu, take him out to eat, just the two of you. Practice ordering off the adult menu in a variety of restaurants. Communicate restaurant etiquette, how to order, what to ask, how to treat a server, and more. Mix well with plenty of conversation and laughter. When your teenager is out with friends he'll already know what to do and can concentrate on the fun of friendship and not wonder what an *hors d'oeuvre* is.

Mature humor: Practice real humor that makes real fun—rather than fun of people. Knowing what to laugh at is an adult skill. Refuse to laugh at demeaning or racial jokes. When your child or teen brings home a tacky joke talk about it: "What's that joke really saying? What would make it better?" Find genuine humor in puns, plays on words, and riddles that build up the intellect as well as the funny bone.

Love that license: Make a big deal out of getting a driver's permit and then a driver's license. Give warnings like "Take care of the car, so you'll take care of the people inside." But along with that, let your teenager know why you trust him in the car: "You drive *well*. Thanks for driving in a way that makes me trust you." As you are impressed, your teen has less need to impress peers by driving wildly.

CHRISTIANS REALLY DO HAVE MORE FUN (CONTINUED)

Save some stuff: Lock-ins were once a rite of passage into the youth department at church. Now young elementary school programs offer them. What's there to wait for? Build the concept of "something new every year" by giving your children one more privilege for each year of life. At six you can choose a two-wheel bike; at eight, arrange your room how you want it; at ten you get to go to summer camp; at eleven you may get your ears pierced; at twelve you can have a slumber party; at thirteen, attend lock-ins; at fifteen budget your own clothes money; and so on.

Party practice: Teach the art of fun with friends. When your daughter has a slumber party, demonstrate how to keep the fun moving with charades, card games, and board games. When your son has friends over for a movie, coach him ahead of time on when to serve popcorn and how to make sure there are enough intermissions. Work together to select and prepare the food, to choose mixers and discussion prompters to pull in reluctant participators.

Privacy paces: As you teach your child to have fun with friends and groups, give progressive privacy. Your six-year-old will need you to give the party. Your ten-year-old will choose his own activities but want you to play or lead some games with the crowd. Your fourteen-year-old will want you nearby to privately ask how to handle lulls. Your seventeen-year-old can often handle entertaining by himself. But even the most mature eighteen-year-old won't be ready if you haven't given instruction all along. And all ages need you in the house, checking in.

Bundles of books: Whether your child is having a birthday party, a sleepover, or a date, find idea books. Rather than reinvent the wheel, learn from other's good experiences with fun. One of the best is *258 Great Dates While You Wait* by Susie Shellenberger and Greg Johnson.

both want to hug her. Yet my memories of those years were clouded by doctor visit after doctor visit. Her ear infections were practically non-stop, and I was nearly frantic in my feelings of helplessness. I remembered her as a baby needing care. Yet here she was a happy person, highly capable of giving to others.

That photo nudged me to notice the fibers of maturity in both my daughters and to help weave those threads into a pattern of mutual care-giving. Certainly when Sarah was two, there were sleepless nights and constant watchfulness. But here was this precious grin I had nearly forgotten. Definitely the teenage years bring roller-coaster craziness. But my Emily displays a humor that keeps me in stitches.

We can embrace the light, or we can bemoan the struggles. We can fan the flickers of selflessness, or we can coddle our children and squash their people-gifts. Show your children how to give joy, then rejoice with them when they do.

Reliving that moment, I imagined myself boosting Sarah's sweetness with, "Pick the one you want to share with Jenny, Sarah."

Sarah gave Jenny a favorite jack-in-the-box.

"Good girl!" I said. "You made Jenny so happy."

A contented Sarah sat next to a happy Jenny, while they continued to play.

Is that what I said? I honestly don't remember. But I can notice what I say today. I can intentionally recognize when Sarah is ready to not only share her possessions but choose which ones to purchase. Together with God I can help her weave compassion and wisdom as she chooses her playmates, builds forever friendships, and chooses a mate from among her friends. I can help her discover a vocational focus, select a college, manage her time, and organize her life, all to the glory of God. Through all this and more she can give joy to others. She can enjoy the best privilege of independence—choosing to care.

Each year our children can do more to bring the answer to Jesus' prayer, "Our Father . . . your kingdom come, your will be done on earth as it is in heaven" (Matthew 6:9–10). Remember? A family that enjoys each other is a family that embodies God's fulfillment of that prayer. But God's genuine love and enjoyment is never confined to the family. The family that touches the world around it spreads His love in a way wildly pleasing to Him. Every time someone obeys God or imitates Jesus, God's kingdom is advanced.

Emily helped it happen just the other day. On her own, without prodding from any adult, she and her friend worked up the courage to invite a new girl to sit with them at their lunch table. Because of their expressed friendship, this girl experienced just what unity in Christ is all about. As an independent teenager Emily accomplished what I could not. We parents can't make teenagers feel at home at school; but Emily and her friend could and did. Their own joy was as deep as that of their new lunch comrade.

Refuse to deny your growing children the joy of making wise choices, of building good friendships, of showing clear kindness, of learning from mistakes. Equip them to do all of these and then let them succeed.

Weave Toward God's Pattern

When Sarah creates a weaving, she starts with a plan of what she'll make and how big it will be. She won't end up with a pillow if she begins with only enough rows for a belt. But she may find that what she thought would be a pillow cover looks better as a purse. We parents must likewise be purposeful in our kids' independence training while opening ourselves to surprises. What kind of adult do you want your child to become? Will he be a man who shows genuine interest in every person he meets? Or a woman who holds firmly to good, quietly doing right, no matter what wrong those around her do? Will he think things through, rather than act on impulse or fear? Will she be able to take complex problems and identify the root cause? Will he make smart choices and work to follow through with them? Will she be able to approach difficulties with peace? Will he seek to gain wisdom rather than possessions? Will she manage time well? Will he manage money wisely? Will she make the most of every day, finding and doing the good God wants her to do? Will he value his wife and delight in each day with her? Will she smile at the sweet togetherness she shares with her family, a togetherness that weathers storms as well as sunshine?

All these things happen not through hoping or dreaming but through day-by-day teaching. If I want my daughter to see the root cause of problems, we'll watch for those together. I'll encourage her when she asks questions rather than push away her questions as bothersome. If I want my son to manage money wisely, I'll give him

BACK-OFF BASICS

Backing off is a step-by-step thing, a series of opportunities to let your teenager succeed on his own. But backing off includes important constants. As you launch a lifetime of learning from God, keep the anchors set fast.

Back off of PROBLEM SOLVING

. . . by mutually listing several options and prompting your teen to choose the ones that will work best. But insist that your teenager be God-honoring, ethical, and honest in the way he solves dilemmas.

Back off of HOMEWORK

. . . by letting your teenager find ways and times to do it himself, by providing an assignment book, by using sticky-notes or another method if assignment books don't work, and by celebrating when it's all done. But continue to insist she do all of it before TV or going out. Stay in touch enough to know that she understands, or that she gets the help she needs from you or a tutor.

Back off of LECTURING

. . . by listening as much as you talk and by asking questions. But continue to express what you believe and why. And affirm your teen's great ideas.

Back off of handing out MONEY

. . . by showing your teen how to manage his own. Give a specific amount to cover lunches, clothes, entertainment, and hobbies. But continue to communicate that there is a budget involved.

BACK-OFF BASICS (CONTINUED)

Back off of packing SUITCASES

. . . for your teen and show him how to go through his routine and get the things he needs while he's away from home: get up, brush teeth (need a toothbrush and paste), get dressed (need change of clothes), put PJs in laundry (need pajamas, laundry bag), and so on. But continue to check the suitcase for what's needed. And show what to do if he does forget something crucial.

Back off of public I-LOVE-YOUs

. . . by saying them in the car or at home. But continue to say I love you privately, and show your love with attention and private hugs.

Back off of NAGGING

"Mom, when you keep telling me what to do I want to do the opposite. There are more factors in this than you realize. Quit pushing!" We parents are not the only ones who are trying to do right. Trust your teenager. But make sure he's living in ways worthy of your trust. Enforce the basics like school and church attendance, completing assignments, keeping commitments, and living ethically.

Back off of DECISION-MAKING

Should I wear the blue T-shirt or the print one? Should I go to the youth council meeting or work with Special Olympics? Should I become a doctor or a nurse? Progressively let your child and teenager make his own wise choices, letting him know that many decisions are between good and best. But continue to identify the consequences of each choice. Talk over what God might be prodding them to do and why.

allowance as a young child and increase it over the years. I'll let him make both wise and foolish choices, and experience on a small scale the wealth and want that result. We'll talk together about how to spend even better next time. Then when he manages his family's money, there will be enough for family needs from marriage to retirement, with a nest egg to spare.

Backing off doesn't mean we back away. We absolutely must continue to express guidance and interest. Teenagers need this more than at any other age. But they need new and different designs. Now, instead of my choosing my children's clothes, we look together through the catalogs and the store racks. Instead of showing my girls how to write a book report, they write it and come to me for editing. Rather than ask about every detail of daily problems, I make myself available and let my daughters bring up what they want to tell me about.

It's not that my job is over; in some ways it's harder now than before. I must sense when to speak and when to be silent. I must discern when to insist that my girls go ahead and complete that book report on a certain day, or when to let them make that judgment. I must know when to ask about a specific area, and when to let it be. And perhaps most importantly I must do all this with an attitude that makes the transition from childhood to independence humorous rather than agonizing.

We begin with a picture of adulthood. Invite God to paint for you a picture of each of your children full grown. Notice colors of personality rather than vocational or activity goals. Seek your child's input; "What kind of adult do you want to be?" "What adults do you admire?" "What do you hope for and dream of?"

With this plan in mind, participate actively with God, your very wise child, and your spouse to create a magnificent tapestry of maturity. Daily discover which fibers will best contribute to Christ-centered independence. Choose the actions, attitudes, and experiences that lead your child toward Christlikeness. Perhaps Paul said it best in his prayer for the Christians at Ephesus:

> For this reason I kneel before the Father, from whom his whole family in heaven and on earth derives its name. I pray that out of his glorious riches he may strengthen you with power through his Spirit in your inner being, so that Christ may dwell

in your hearts through faith. And I pray that you, being rooted and established in love, may have power, together with all the saints, to grasp how wide and long and high and deep is the love of Christ and to know this love that surpasses knowledge—that you may be filled to the measure of all the fullness of God.

Ephesians 3:14–19

This indescribable good comes through the nitty-gritty of life. When my girls were young teenagers, they were especially self-conscious of anything I said when a peer or another adult was around. Questions I could ask unimpeded on any other day, like, "How did the test go?" came across as reproachful reprimands. Teasing could look like failure to take them seriously. Were my children being selfish and moody? Not at all. They were conscious of the need to appear competent and lovable around these valued friends. My girls were mature enough to recognize that they stand on their own, that their goodness in Christ is something they must develop, not something I can impart to them. Their sensitivity meant the desire to do right, not the avoidance of it.

This prompted me to watch my words so I could weave confidence into their maturity pattern. I deliberately paid attention to signs of self-consciousness, so I could say less instead of more. I moved to the background to give them opportunities to display and refine their people skills. I recognized these critical junctures not as stages, but as opportunities to be supportive rather than smotherish. This didn't come without disaster. Many were the times I said too much or responded in ways that squashed my children's confidence. Too often I controlled the circumstances rather than letting my children lead. Thankfully, neither my children nor my Lord have given up on me.

God continues to teach me how to look at all the colors and pick just the ones to match the current pattern. How? I look at God's finished weaving. What color action on my part will best prompt my daughter to grow love, joy, peace, patience, kindness, goodness, gentleness, faithfulness, and self control for a lifetime? (Galatians 5:22–23) Will the pattern be stronger if I speak or stay silent? If I offer information or simply listen? If I nudge her to go to the event or let her make her own choice? If I show her how to manage or let her discover that for herself? If I assure her or simply hear her worries?

If I restrict her or prompt her? There's a time for all of these. Invite the Master to guide your hand, to discover which to use:

> There is a time for everything,
> and a season for every activity under heaven . . .
> a time to plant and a time to uproot . . .
> a time to weep and a time to laugh,
> a time to mourn and a time to dance . . .
> a time to embrace and a time to refrain . . .
> a time to be silent and a time to speak.
> Ecclesiastes 3:1, 2b, 4, 5b, 7b

Work on the Warp Threads

As God guides you, build a loom of virtue for your children to weave their lives on. The most important virtues are the simple things—kindness, understanding, wisdom, treating others as you'd want to be treated. These are not simple to do, but are simply powerful. Friendship, family, work, play, free time, decisions—all weave more colorfully when simple care is expressed. In fact, there's not a single area of life that's not enhanced with daily thoughtfulness. Passionately insist that your children be considerate, display understanding, be thoughtful, and treat others as they want to be treated. Then express the same godly virtues as you care for your children.

Your teenager will thank you forever if you use simple care to understand him. He feels things deeply, both joy and agony, and he needs someone to understand and validate those feelings. Hear what your teenager feels and help him discover what to do about those feelings. When your son says, "I don't want to teach Bible School next week," it's not that he's unspiritual. It means he just got home from a mission trip and needs some down time. Suggest, "Wait a day

> Think of one area of life that wouldn't be helped with kindness, understanding, thoughtfulness, and treating others as you'd want to be treated.

and then see how you're doing" rather than accuse with "You'd better pray about that attitude!" Remember to direct him to sleep and eat, as we saw God did for tired Elijah (1 Kings 19:5–8). Assure him that his renewing rest honors God just as powerfully as the mission trip did the week before. Once he has a weekend to just *be*, he'll likely choose to teach Bible School. And even if he goes reluctantly, you'll hear a whole new story when he returns home: delight over his fascinating students.

Feel what your teenagers feel whether they're delighted or devastated. The Bible urges us to "rejoice with those who rejoice; mourn with those who mourn" (Romans 12:15). Teenagers do a lot of both. They rejoice when they make the yearbook staff or a special someone gives them attention. They mourn when they fail a test or when someone close to them suffers. They both rejoice and mourn at the realization that they will soon be on their own. When your teen knows somebody understands, he can manage almost anything. This happened to Sarah and me one summer afternoon.

"They think it's spread," said Sarah's teacher, one of the most precious friends in our lives. She had telephoned to give us the results of her post-chemotherapy tests.

"Oh, I hate cancer." I said. Tears threatened to spill over. *I need to be strong for her*, I thought. Then, as though nudged from God, I remembered six years earlier when my good friend Sandy had cried along with me on the day of my Emily's cancer diagnosis. Sandy's tears powerfully showed me that she cared too. They were my favorite expression of care on that sad day. *Why am I trying to hold it back? Marie matters to me, and as I cry I can let her know that.*

So I let the tears come, and Marie cried too. It was awkward but comforting. Together we wept and mustered strength for her next cancer battle.

After hanging up the phone I struggled to get it together enough to tell Sarah. As I sighed deeply, I once again realized, *No, I don't have to get it together first. Sarah and I can weep together.* So I took a breath and headed for Sarah's room, where she was happily arranging her stuffed gorillas to make room for her latest adoptee.

"I've got sad news. Marie's cancer has spread instead of disappeared," I said, starting to cry again. "It makes me really sad."

Sarah stood motionless for a few seconds, seconds that seemed like eternity. I wondered if I'd done the right thing. Then, confused, she asked, "But why did it come back? Emily's didn't do that."

"Well, they know more about fighting children's cancers than adult ones. Adult cancers are somehow harder to stop. And the kind Marie has is really mean," I explained, realizing Sarah didn't want an explanation as much as she wanted Marie's cancer to go away. "We'll help Marie fight."

"But what if she feels too sick to teach?" said Sarah, conscious of how deeply she depended on Marie's skills.

"She'll take a break and then come back when she feels better," I suggested.

"But I don't want Marie to die!" Sarah stressed. Marie, not her skills or actions, was who really mattered.

"Me either," I said as we hugged and cried. "And this doesn't mean she will. Do you want to talk to God about it?"

"Yes," Sarah said. "But I don't want to say anything. You do it."

So I voiced our prayer for a successful fight against the cancer we hated.

Thirty minutes later Sarah was outside with friends. You'd never know she was hurting. That's the nature of young grief—intense and then over.

Does brevity mean it wasn't worth feeling? Not at all. Feeling it is what moved Sarah on through it. Your teenager will be similar. Once he knows someone cares, he'll be ready to face any problem head on. This doesn't mean problems are instantly over when we feel them, or that feeling them is enough to solve them. It means that grief is the first step and an un-skipable one. Sarah grieved many more times with and for her teacher. The waves of grief came in intense snatches, flowing in an uneasy mix with joy. As she fully felt the pain, she grew ready to decide what to do about it.

As your teenager decides what to do, point him toward God. He will help your teen discover how to meet the need behind the feelings. Does your discouraged teenager need to approach the next test a bit differently, perhaps working the easier problems first so the harder ones won't keep him from completing the test? How will your ecstatic teen celebrate the yearbook position? When will your teen care for others in the midst of her grief? God is the best one to help with this. He will not only show your teenager what to do about his feelings, but give him the love and power to take those steps.

For Sarah this meant sitting quietly and feeling sad, snuggled up in God's blanket of care. It also meant praying and writing. At first Sarah didn't have words for her prayers. As in Romans 8:26, the Holy Spirit interceded for her. Later she expressed her prayers eloquently, speaking of her anger, her anguish, and her hope. Some of her prayers were spoken, but most were written in a journal with colors to match her feelings. Finally it meant decorating a cake for Marie with the words "Boo-hoo! Marie's cancer did not go!" It was a bittersweet acknowledgement that Marie matters, that we don't have to explain away the pain. With the silly almost-rhyme on the cake, Sarah could cheer her teacher and share her anguish. The two spoke of hope, and of their anger at the mean disease called cancer. Neither knew what the future held, but both knew they'd stick with each other no matter what.

Taking God-guided action shows your teen that he isn't powerless, that he can always do something to make a situation better or more manageable. When your teenager studies better his grade goes up a little. When he celebrates his yearbook position with his fellow staffers, they build a bond that gets them ready for working together. When she cares for a grieving friend, both feel beter. This recognition that God wants to work through him is crucial to teenagers. Your teen must know he has power both to celebrate and to make it through the pain. He must discover that real power comes only through God, and is freely available to him. Without God's power he will seek power through fast driving, angry words, rejection of all who care, and other bogus forces.

No matter how agonizing, walk through sadness with your teenager. It won't be as easy as walking through the happy times. But both will bring you closer. Sharing the events in your teenager's life will seal a bond of togetherness that will last long after he's out on his own. Whether it's the single-day sadness that comes through an unfair homework assignment, or the lifelong sadness that comes from an unfair disability, hear and understand your child's sad times. Whether it's the hour-long happiness that comes through eating in a favorite restaurant or the year-long delight of a great Sunday school teacher, hear and celebrate your child's good times.

Then refuse to keep this sharing to yourself. Cultivate a caring habit in your kids. Emily is tremendously sensitive in helping Sarah with her grief, and with celebrating her joys. Sarah listens with rapt attention to the details of Emily's victories and sorrows. They fre-

TRENCH TRAINING

True spirituality works in the good and bad, the easy and hard of life. Prepare your children to live hand-in-hand with God. Some ways to do this:

Welcome Questions: As your child moves from baby food to meat, from inherited faith to personal faith, she will ask: "How do you know God is real?" "Am I bad if I'm tempted?" "How do I know God's will in this?" Welcome questions as steps toward mature faith. Answer honestly and with Scriptures. And don't be afraid to say you're still learning the answer to that question yourself.

Walk Your Talk, Talk Your Walk: One of the best ways your children will learn spiritual maturity is to see it in you. So do what you say you believe. And say why you do what you do. If you want your children to love people, refuse to gossip about them. If you want them to learn forgiveness, forgive them. If you want your child to handle anger well, do so yourself.

Find Spiritual Gifts: Notice what's unique and wonderful about your children. Then search passages like Romans 12, 1 Corinthians 12–13, and Ephesians 4 to discover what your children's spiritual gifts may be. "You understand people's feelings so well. You may have the spiritual gift of encouragement." When children see themselves as uniquely gifted by God, they are more likely to live that gift in His honor. As you talk about spiritual gifts in the course of the day, your children see gifts as something to live continually.

Love God Rather Than Use Him: "Please pray that I get to use the car Friday; my parents haven't let me drive since I got that speeding ticket," asked Pete. Sounds real spiritual, but Pete is using God to get what Pete wants.

TRENCH TRAINING (CONTINUED)

Be Sad Without Whining: Some things are just sad—disabilities, cancer, catastrophe, failed tests. Refuse to call these good, but equally refuse to use them as an excuse for self-pity. Equip your child to be sad without whining, to do good in the midst of his anguish (Romans 12:15; 1 Peter 4:19). See Chapter 7 for ideas.

Be Happy Without Gloating: When good things happen, say, "Don't sing a song about it" (you know the song: "*Nah-nah-nah-nah-nah-nah*, I got ice cream and you didn't"). It's a gentle reminder not to compare your goods or bads in a divisive way.

Jump for Joy: Affirm your children for enjoying themselves in good ways. Never laugh at children who do mean or selfish things. Always laugh with children who enjoy the simple things in loving ways: "You three are having such fun climbing that tree. Didn't God do well when He created trees!"

Talk about Life with a Spiritual Perspective: Communicate spirituality as a day-by-day honoring of God, the reason all our efforts make sense. Even the way your child brushes his teeth can honor God. "Thanks for sharing the sink with your brother so patiently; that's true love" (Galatians 5:22–23).

Love in the Trenches: The most powerful witness is loving actions. Your child can remain a friend when others climb the social ladder. He can tell the truth no matter how many other people lie. She can quietly do good even when others laugh at good. When a friend is attacked or belittled, your child can turn the attack to admiration. Then they can use words to tell why—and in Whose honor—they do all this. It's seldom easy—admit that. But assure your children that they can do the right thing without looking weird. How do you know? Because Jesus lived on earth and did exactly that.

quently teach me how to share pain as well as joy. And they show me how much more powerfully happy we become when we go through life together.

> Two are better than one,
>   because they have a good return for their work:
> If one falls down,
>   his friend can help him up! . . .
> Though one may be overpowered,
>   two can defend themselves.
> A cord of three strands is not quickly broken.
> Ecclesiastes 4:9–10, 12

Pass the Shuttle

Letting my children go becomes easier when I recognize that I'm not the center of my child's joy-giving and joy-receiving. God is. Neither my children nor yours will ever be fully independent. They'll always need God. Long after our children leave home they'll still be learning lessons in joy-giving and joy-receiving.

In light of this, pushing away is a compliment. It means our children are ready to plait together fibers of independence and design their own joy. It means they can responsibly weave on their own with God as their guide.

My head knows this, but my heart struggles. Giving my children independence is anything but easy for me. I'm the mom who kept care checklists from the time my children were infants, who ran the forgotten lunch to elementary school, who preferred everyone play at my house so I could keep an eye on them. Because I know this about myself, I admit that it's hard for me to let my children go. Then I deliberately listen when my daughter says, "Let me handle it, Mom. I know what I'm doing." I meet her need and not my own.

My friend Martha has the opposite problem. She assumes that what she doesn't know won't hurt her. She finds it easier to let her sons and daughter do what they want, rather than guide them to form Christlike patterns. Still in elementary school, her sons are often outside until midnight. Why? Because they want to. Her daughter behaves rudely at school and church, refusing to participate if she's not in the mood. Martha's daughter says the same thing mine does, "Let me handle it. I know what I'm doing." But the words mean something entirely different.

Move toward the middle of Martha and me, to the center of freedom and goodness. Together with God weave in your children life management skills such as friendship, resourcefulness, decision-making, and people-valuing. Discover the best pace to give each of your children freedom to try to succeed at weaving their lives. Know that they'll have to remove a thread and try again from time to time. But the final pattern will be a masterpiece they'll give with pleasure.

Joyfully, and together with your children, live God's truth in ways that build a family fabric, a blanket of joy that is passed down from generation to generation. And bank on God's very personal promise: "I will instruct you and teach you in the way you should go; I will counsel you and watch over you" (Psalm 32:8).

Joy Tip

Deliberately guide your children toward independence, wrapping them in a tapestry of God-centered competence and confidence. Daily weave a colorful pattern of how-to's and why-for's that equip your children to take their place in this world and in eternity. Then keep warm with the mutuality of adult relationships.

9

SO HOW DO I DO ALL OF THIS?

Let love and faithfulness never leave you; bind them around your neck, write them on the tablet of your heart. Then you will win favor and a good name in the sight of God and man.

—Proverbs 3:3–4

Raising a family of friends will remain a wishful thought unless you know some practical secrets to reshaping attitudes and creating memories. Besides the skills and suggestions you've already read throughout this book, here are additional quick ideas to use daily. Remember that what works with a two-year-old might be the very same idea that works with a twenty-two-year-old. But more often, some ideas will work best with one child and others with another. Custom design and adapt these ideas to fit the personalities and needs of each of your one-of-a-kind children. Rather than worry about which idea is exactly right, try several and watch how your child responds. Then repeat the ones that bring the greatest joy.

Fun During Chores

Agree that nobody likes doing chores—that's why they're called chores. But clothes have to be washed and the lawn has to be mowed. So split up the work to give everybody more time to pursue more pleasant activities. Then cultivate the habit of each family member thanking the other for doing chores well so each can have more time.

- *Picture This:* Offer checklists for multi-step chores when teaching a chore for the first time. A clean bedroom includes picking up paper, putting books away, straightening the dresser, dusting, and vacuuming. Make the list in picture or rebus form for pre-readers.

- *Music to Clean to:* Play your child's favorite music and dub it "Clean Up Music." The beat of your teenagers' contemporary Christian music can make everyone's chore attitude bouncier (HINT: Christian music isn't soft versus loud, country versus rock. It's any musical style that tells the truth and encourages good living. Refuse to cheat yourself by saving Christian music for Sundays. Play Christian music exclusively from the time your children are babies.)

- *Quiz Me:* Make studying more fun by encouraging siblings to quiz each other. Help them balance their time so one doesn't lose all his study time to the other. A load of homework can make children feel oppressed and powerless. Being the quiz authority for siblings helps children feel empowered and ready to master their own studies.

- *Project Photos:* As soon as school maps or drama dioramas are completed, eagerly shoot pictures of them. Knowing the project is worth photographing prompts your child to do a good job and put that last little effort in when motivation is waning.

- *Pressure Paces:* Relieve some of the stress of exams or big tests by giving your child steps to achieve: (1) after you finish memorizing the definitions you can get a piece of bubble gum; (2) after I quiz you on content you can go outside and swing for five minutes; (3) after you read the whole chapter once more you can take your shower; (4) then, tomorrow after you take the exam we'll go out for a frozen lemonade.

- *You Help Me:* Invite your reluctant-to-practice-piano child to play a concert for you while you clean the bathroom. "This is my least favorite chore, but when you play music for me it seems like no work at all."

- *Here's Why:* Challenge your children to find the reason for every job that needs doing, and a good in the doing of it. If you turn challenge to a contest, your children will likely outdo you.

- *As-You's:* Eliminate big chores with "as-you's": Everybody carry clothes to the hamper *as you* change. Everybody carry your own dishes to the sink *as you* leave the table or family room. Everybody wipe up the sink *as you* finish using it. Everybody wipe your feet *as you* enter the house.

- *A Better Way:* Hold a weekly inventiveness challenge. Whoever discovers a unique or more interesting way to do a chore gets to choose the menu for the night of their choice. The family member who does the laundry might discover a new *as-you* that would help. The one who takes out the garbage might suggest looking for an outdoor blessing as you trek to the trash can. The little sister who feels like her brother isn't doing his *as-you's* might come up with a funny-but-want-to-avoid-it punishment for non-chore-doers.

- *Chore Coupons:* To keep one member from overusing another's kindness, use chore coupons. Assign each chore a coupon value. Mowing the lawn might be worth five coupons if taking out the garbage is worth one coupon. Award each family member five coupons to start. Your teenager might use all five coupons when he has exams and must enlist his sister to do his chores. He can earn those coupons back by doing her chores the week she has nightly play practice. Parents must use coupons too.

- *It's Your Draw:* Divide chores by favorites where possible. You might prefer washing the clothes while your teenager prefers folding. But for those chores nobody likes or everybody likes, use a chore box. Together with your family, write regular chores on individual slips of paper. Combine short chores to equal the time and effort of larger chores. Then, daily, each family member draws and completes an equal number of chores. Trading is allowed only on days that start with a T.

- *Reward at the End:* Use chore charts for young children. Let children add a sticker each time they finish a chore. Even older teenagers might enjoy adding check marks if a reward comes at the end—a reward like an evening alone with you.

- *Clock Check:* Race against the clock to complete particularly tedious chores. Race against each other to make everyone's chores more fun.

Fun While Separated

Family is family even when separated by camp, college, and crazy schedules. Find ways to keep togetherness strong even across the miles.

- *Voice From Home:* Leave messages on your college student's answering machine to find when she returns from that particularly hard test.
- *Fat Letters:* Send a tiny teddy bear in an envelope to your ten-year-old at camp. Attach a tag that says the bear is bringing hugs from home.
- *Arrival-Day Greetings:* Write a letter and mail it a day or two before your child leaves for camp or college so she'll get a letter on arrival day.
- *Paper Possibilities:* Find a different medium to write on each time you write a letter. Inventive possibilities include a paper lunch sack, a scrap of cloth from the dress you had such fun making together, a napkin from the restaurant where you shared that fun meal—or where you'd like to eat together next time. Ready-made stationery papers work well too—look for a variety of shapes, sizes, and textures.
- *Catchy Closures:* Begin and close letters a different way each time you write, or vary your child's favorites. Possible greetings include:
    - *—"Dear best student in the world"*
    - *—"To my favorite first daughter"*
    - *—"Greetings to the son who makes me smile"*
    - *—"Hi, expert friend-maker"*
    - *—"Hello on this good day that God has made"*

  Try closures like:
    - *—"From your dad who cares about everything that happens to you"*
    - *—"Hugs from your mom and your friend"*
    - *—"Bye for now and remember that I'm glad God made us a family"*
    - *—"From the one who admires your positive spirit"*
    - *—"Grace and peace to you"* (the apostle Paul liked this one! See it in Romans 1:7, Galatians 1:3, and more).

  When I went to college my grandfather signed his letters a different way every week for a year. I eagerly anticipated each letter and read the closures first. I still have those signatures in an envelope in my attic.
- *Flowers Good Enough to Eat:* Send a bouquet of cookies to your

soldier, your college student, or to your child in the hospital. Companies create them or you can make your own and perch each cookie on a stick stuck into a pot. Wrap the bunch in brightly colored wrapping papers. Choose your child's favorite recipe or shape the cookies to reflect your child's favorite activities. Shape a baseball bat, glove, and ball for your baseball player. Shape a pickle, teddy bear, and book for your avid reader who collects teddy bears and munches on pickles.

- *Box of Love:* Send care packages to your away-from-home child or teenager. Include favorite snacks, home-baked goodies, books in a favorite series, contemporary Christian music tapes, new pieces for a collection (baseball cards, figurines, and more), whatever simple gifts would delight your child. Time the arrival of the package for an occasion like final exams, laundry day, or another needs-something-fun occasion.

Fun On Trips

The trip really can be as fun as the destination. Says a real live young teenager, "I really enjoy those long car rides because you can listen to music and do stuff without interruption."

- *Book of Fun:* Guide each child to use a blank vinyl notebook and a variety of papers, stickers, and supplies to make a travel notebook. Your older children and teenagers can decorate the outside with paint pens and fill the inside with a variety of papers, markers, pencils, and pens. Sample items to include: graph paper to draw a scale robot or cross-stitch patterns, sticky paper to make paper doll clothes or animal figures, shiny paper to make 3-D scenes, origami paper to make origami sculptures, school paper to keep a trip journal, multicolor pens or pencils to make the drawing and writing more fun, unusual markers such as color-change ones or sparkly ones to make unique pictures, stickers of all varieties to add figures to drawn scenes, or to stick for the pure fun of it. Offer a pouch for the little things and a three-hole punch to insert the papers.
- *Trip Countdown Chain:* Direct your kids to make a paper chain with one link for every day until the trip. Write on each link an action to prepare for travel such as: pack my clothes, gather

stamps and addresses for writing friends, call someone to take my role in the church event I'll miss, make my travel notebook, pack the travel games. Each day your children remove one link and do that preparation.

- *Trip Chain:* Make a second chain for use in the car. This chain includes a link for every hour on the road. On these links write an activity to make the travel more interesting. Ideas include: Listen to a new Christian music tape, write postcards to friends, play a travel game, quiz my parents on things I've always wanted to ask but never had time to ask, ask for a top-of-the-hour surprise (see next idea).

- *Top-of-the-Hour Fun:* Pack a new activity for each hour you'll be on the road or in the air. Possibilities include new books in your child's favorite series, a new Christian music tape, a new travel game, a fun snack that takes a long time to eat (like candy neck-laces or pouches of tiny gum), something to put in the travel notebook, a do-in-the-car construction toy or stitchery kit, a non-material suggestion such as listing for each letter of the alphabet a different thing you're thankful for on this trip. HINT: If your children make a *Trip Chain* (previous idea), alternate with them to provide the hourly activity.

- *Plan Surprises:* Let siblings help select top-of-the-hour fun sur-prises. Give each sibling an amount of surprises to find, along with strict instructions to show their discoveries to no one but you. Refuse to limit activity shopping to the toy aisle. Explore the school supply aisle, craft section, even the clothes clearance table where you might find bargain socks for making puppets or silly hats for in-the-car dramas. Watch for fun pens, puzzle books, fancily shaped notebooks, stickers, papers, activities, and more. Have fun hiding these surprises from each other both in the store and in the car. Then in the car, take turns with your children to present the surprises.

- *Preparation Shop:* Because they can only eat them in the car, choosing travel snacks generates excitement for the car ride. Shop together for these snacks. Similar to *Plan Surprises*, let each child pick an item or two. Urge your children to choose foods that would appeal to all family members, or at least bal-ance them—adults may not adore gummy candy with the same enthusiasm children do; small children risk choking if they munch the trail mix adults enjoy. You may want to keep these snacks secret and let each child check them out independently, with you in close proximity for younger children.

- *Surprise Tape:* On the busy day when you're completing your final packing, offer blank cassette tapes and a recorder for children to make their own trip tapes. They might sing songs, speak riddles, or create a mystery for your listening family to solve.

- *Dimes on the Dashboard:* This technique virtually eliminates car bickering. Display for each child a row of ten dimes. Explain that you'll take away one dime every time they say an unkind word or show an uncooperative attitude. At the end of each hundred miles they can keep whatever dimes are left and start with ten fresh dimes. They can use earned dimes for vending machines or souvenir spending. For the next 100 miles, offer the option of five quarters. This yields more payoff at the end but greater loss for bickering. The friend who shared this marvelous tip said he removed a set of dimes when his daughters began to squabble. He then removed another when they complained about losing dimes. He didn't have to remove a third.

- *Personal Cameras:* Give each child his or her own camera to capture memories of the trip. Simple point-and-shoot cameras are inexpensive and produce surprisingly good quality prints. Even an older preschooler can handle a camera if shown how (you'll need to keep up with it). (The cardboard ones you give up when you put the film in for developing are great for very young children.)

- *Plentiful Snapshots:* Take a camera of your own too. Generously take shots of everything. We once shot six rolls of film at Disney World, which gave us the luxury of choosing good shots from the not-so-good ones. Even the off-center and blurry photos prompted generous memories and hilarious laughter. Film and developing are inexpensive if you buy your film in discount stores rather than gift shops, and if you avoid the overnight and ready-in-an-hour developing places. Consider taking along a film mailer with a check already filled out. Then drop your first couple rolls of film in the mail as soon as you complete them. Your pictures will greet you when you return home.

Hotel Fun

No bed is as good as the one at home, but hotels provide opportunities for not-to-be-missed adventures. Simply sleeping in one big room provides grand fun for children.

- *Hotel Haven:* Call ahead to ensure the little things that make your stay fun. Suppose you and grandparents are traveling together and really want adjoining rooms. Many hotel chains can't guarantee these until the day of arrival. Call that morning and kindly request adjoining rooms. They'll usually go ahead and put you in those rooms and give you the room number.
- *Comfy and Close:* Occasionally rent a hotel room with a king-size bed so the whole family can pile in the same bed for a single night. Expect bumpy sleep but great stories to tell for generations to come: "I slept all night with an elbow in my ear!" "Wasn't it cuddly to watch that movie all in the same bed!"
- *Shared Reading:* Purchase book lights for every member. Turn out all the lights and read your books together in the dark while snuggled in bed.
- *Take Care of Details:* Let the youngest member go with the oldest one to get the ice for the ice bucket. Let each child take turns unlocking the door with the neat credit-card-like key that makes a special beep. Assign someone to check the room before departing to be sure you got everything. Another can divide up the paper and shampoo samples. Still another can phone in the request for a wake-up call.
- *Up With the Clock:* Your offspring might not sleep as late as you'd like to and you might not get up as early as your children would like. To hit a happy medium, provide a book and a time for quiet rising. "You may not move until the clock says seven-oh-oh. Then you can use your book light to read."

Enjoyment in the Hospital

The hospital isn't typically a place of happiness. But God pokes joy into every situation. Work along with Him as you bring smiles and steady love to the sickroom.

- *Make Friends:* If your child has a regular doctor visit for allergy shots, for vision check-ups, or for chemotherapy, get to know the others who wait. Talking while you play games like UNO®™ will help make this more comfortable. Then going to the doctor can be like old home week, a reunion with friends you're glad to see.

- *It'll Cost You:* Let your hospitalized child post a sign on the door that says "25¢ for every shot; 50¢ if you take blood or other specimens back out with you." See how many care-givers comply.
- *Music and Magazines:* Bring your child's favorite Christian music, magazines, and books to help him get his mind off the pain and chaos of hospitalization. If your child faces chronic illness, keep the latest magazine issue in a hospital bag until the next one comes. Then you'll always have a new one on hand. Bring a personal stereo to play the music.
- *Custom Design:* Make the hospital room your child's own with helium balloons, streamers, and her art. Display cards from friends and relatives. Get permission to hang things from the ceiling as well as display on the walls. Hang things upside down and at crazy angles to give your child some intriguing reading.
- *Playroom:* Find and make good use of the hospital playroom. From crafts to make to shows to attend, from visitors to meet to toys to check out, playrooms are a declaration that illness doesn't have to stop joy. Even your teenagers will enjoy activities especially designed for them. Especially for non-emergency visits, select a hospital with a good playroom and caring personnel.
- *Present-a-Day:* Gather all the gifts people bring in one big box. Wrap the ones that don't come wrapped. Then let your child open one a day. This strategy spreads out the fun and makes each day one to look forward to. If painful procedures are part of the day, you might open the gifts immediately after that.

Fun While Waiting

Waiting. Hospitals aren't the only places we have to wait. It happens at church potluck dinners and at the orthodontist. It happens in traffic jams and in airports. Sometimes you can plan for it. Other times it's a surprise. Make the most of down time with ideas like the following:

- *Paper Preparedness*: Keep a notepad and pen in your purse or pocket at all times. This can become a hangman pad, origami paper, stationery, a tent for imaginary figures, songwriting paper, and much more. Bringing a ballpoint pen with multiple colors adds to the possibilities.
- *Tale Telling*: Being stuck in traffic gives uninterrupted time. Take advantage of it by telling stories about your family. Invite each car passenger to tell one story before any tells a second. Don't be afraid of silence between stories while each child thinks— enjoy savoring the story just told. Definitely tell stories that make each child feel cherished—none that ridicule.
- *I Spy and More*: Brush up on sitting games and create your own. You might make a game with successive clues. First your child would say, "I spy something red." If you guess wrong, she says, "I spy something red with a roundish shape." If still unsuccessful, she would add, "I spy something red with a roundish shape that wiggles." Your child earns a point for every detail she adds before you guess correctly. Sitting games can be played in traffic jams as well as waiting rooms.
- *Sitting Stash*: Keep a box in which you and your family stash "to do's" for that week. Take this box along for scheduled waits such as when one brother waits for the other at Tuesday's soccer practice. Your son might complete his assigned reading while you prepare your Sunday school lesson. Or together you might untangle the fishing line that got jumbled on the last trip.
- *Packed Purse*: Keep stickers, joke books, magazines, and other samples of your child's favorite activity in your purse or car as space allows. Pipe cleaners and paper clips are two unlikely items that provide fun entertainment: sculpt with them, string them together, create jewelry, and more.
- *Homework*: Though your children won't automatically identify homework as fun, it yields fun in the long run. After all, if you do your homework while waiting for allergy shots or during Angela's ball practice, you won't have to do it at home. And there's plenty of fun at home that's not available in waiting rooms.

Fun On Special Days

Each day is a celebration of life, but some days carry unique significance. Custom-design these days with activities and traditions made especially for your family.

- *School's Out Celebration:* Allow each child to invite one friend home on the last day of school to celebrate the advent of summer. Start a traditional meal, like a backyard barbecue or a trip to your kids' favorite restaurant. Set up the backyard pool or sprinkler, break out the frozen treats, and start a summer jigsaw puzzle. Launch your children's favorite summer activities on this day.

- *Twelve Days of Christmas:* Choose twelve stocking-stuffer-type gifts to open, one each day of the twelve days before Christmas. This spreads out the fun. Especially appropriate are seasonal gifts like jingle bell shoelaces or a Christmas tie.

- *Gifts That Last Forever:* Give non-material gifts along with the material ones for Christmas and birthdays. Let your children take turns choosing the gift sentence such as: "What I appreciate about you is . . ."; "A nice thing you do for us as a family is . . ."; "For you this year I hope . . ." and more.

- *You Were Born!* Make a *big* deal over birthdays. Cook the birthday person's favorite foods. Decorate the house with balloons, kid-made posters, streamers, and more. Plan to let the person know what you like about them (See *Gifts That Last Forever*). Let the planning be as fun as the day itself.

- *A Friend for Me Too:* Let each sibling of the birthday boy or girl invite a friend over during the party. These friend pairs can help give the party (even seven-year-olds can help set the table and serve party foods) and can keep each other company while the party's going on. Together with your children, work out ahead of time which parts of the party siblings will attend and which parts they won't. A balance gives both birthday child and sibling opportunity to give time to the other. The non-birthday children feel less left out and the birthday child has more privacy.

- *Planning Is as Fun as the Party:* Avoid surprise parties for children. They enjoy the planning as much or more than the party itself. Begin surprise parties at age fifteen or sixteen.

- *Sweetness Present:* While preserving the center-of-attention spot for the birthday child, do choose one gift for each non-birthday sibling. Keep sweetness and grump points all day. If the sweetness points outnumber the grump points at bedtime, award the gift. Explain this, of course, at the beginning of the day.

- *Separate Privacy:* When one child has a friend over, let the other have a friend too. They'll be more likely to give each other privacy and they'll all enjoy the afternoon more. WARNING: One shortfall—sometimes the younger friends admire the older brother or sister and want to be with them instead. You decide in this case, the one who insists that each pair play separately for a while between being together.

- *Confetti Eggs:* Our family uses these at Easter but they would be fun for any holiday. Blow out raw eggs to leave only the shells. Wash the shells thoroughly, dry for several days, and then fill with confetti. Tape the holes shut with clear tape. On celebration day, divide the eggs evenly. Position yourselves in a large circle and then say GO! Semi-gently smash the eggs on each other's heads and enjoy the flying confetti.

- *New Holidays:* Together with your children, sit down on New Year's Day and create a holiday for each month of the coming year. Ice-cream-on-the-icy-day might come in February. Out-of-school-day might come in June. Birthdays of family members will cover some of the months. Unholiday might cover another. Celebration days unique to your family build a bond of closeness. A spirit of celebration builds anticipation for the year as well as communicates that routine life is worth celebrating.

Make Every Day Special

Why restrict fun to Christmas and birthdays? Children, especially young ones, see each day as an adventure. That's why they rise so early and resist bedtime so firmly. They want to live each moment. Even days like Christmas don't always outdo the joy of an average day. Make it harder for your child to outgrow this delightful characteristic by seeing something good in each day yourself. Find reasons to celebrate plain old Tuesday.

- *Blessing Watch:* Encourage your children to watch for the blessings in that day. "What special happening do you think God will bring to this day?" God's blessings aren't limited to the sensational: watch for the first flower of spring, an encouraging smile from a friend, a recovery from a sore throat, the confidence to speak to someone new, the courage to listen instead of talk, a teacher who communicates clearly, a happy afternoon. Then at bedtime, take a minute to review all the blessings you saw. Blessing watch grows a pattern of expectation and thankfulness.

- *Here's How You Blessed Me:* Help your children recognize their roles in God's plan by pointing out ways He blesses you through them. "Your cheerful whistling has reminded me that we can make it through this tight time." "You always get up right when I wake you in the morning. That saves both of us hassle. Thanks."

- *Here's Me:* Offer your child an hour of your uninterrupted time. Let the answering machine get the phone, don't answer the door, and let the projects rest. "What would you like to do? I'm yours for an hour."

- *Frozen Lemonade on the First:* On the first day of the last month of school, take your children for a frozen lemonade or other simple treat they enjoy. Talk about the school year, what you'll miss, what you'll be glad to let go. Congratulate your children for their hard work and specific successes. This simple venture can energize them for the final stretch.

- *Special-Day Plate:* Purchase a plate (or let your child make one with a factory kit that seals his drawing in a plastic plate) that all identify as the special-day plate. Take turns deciding who to give the plate to every night and why. Perhaps the special plate goes to the child who found the first clover of the spring season. Maybe it goes to the one who's been sick and is better now, or has been sick but has kept his sweet disposition. Finding a reason to celebrate with every meal helps children look for the small blessings in each day.

- *Catalog Captivators:* Constantly watch catalogs, toy stores, even hardware store aisles for fascinating projects that appeal to your children. Then fill your closet or cedar chest with baskets to weave, T-shirts to paint, candles to create, dollhouses to paint, rugs to hook, models to build, books to write, sock monkeys to sew, cross-stitch to design, old fashioned games to play. We once found a kit for Ukrainian Easter eggs—a wax and dye process that took an entire day to do two eggs. But the eggs are heirlooms created on an unexpected snow day. Because the kit was in my closet, we had something to do. Remember to keep your children's specific interests in mind. One of my daughters prefers do-in-a-day projects. The other likes ones that last longer.

Enjoy Relatives

Kin doesn't automatically equal close. Relationships with relatives must be grown just like any friendship. Appreciate and grow through the uniqueness of each relative with actions like these:

- *Tell Me a Story About You:* Cultivate the habit of storytelling. You might begin one Christmas Eve by inviting each member to tell a favorite Christmas memory. Encourage close attention from all family members and resist firmly the temptation to interrupt. Let the storyteller have the floor. Equalize bubbly talkers with shy speakers with a three-sentence limit, followed by four sentences the next round. Young members may want to draw a picture to go along with their story. Favorite birthday memories or "I was so excited/embarrassed when" are other good story starters. As you try structured methods like these, storytelling will begin to naturally pepper conversations. Fervently avoid stories that ridicule or encourage members to laugh at one another. Instead, choose stories that deepen feelings of family belonging and a sense of family history.
- *The Ties That Bind:* Prepare activities that bridge age gaps and time gaps. A group of cousins who see each other once every two years won't find it easy to start talking when they get together. A board game can break the ice. Aged aunts and active preschoolers might enjoy setting the table or decorating the birthday cake together.
- *News We Can Use:* Gather cousins and challenge them to create a holiday newspaper, reporting findings on the paper you provide. Encourage illustrations and provide an instant camera for photographs. Divide responsibilities according to age and abilities, giving more extensive assignments to older cousins, but exclaiming equally over all efforts. A starting list for a Thanks-

giving Day paper: *Memories* of earlier Thanksgivings, gathered from every member present . . . *Food News*, including today's menu and the favorite item of every member . . . *Weather News*, and what kind of weather each member likes . . . *Sports News*, including the televised football game, and today's firsthand activities.

- *Sit at the Kids' Table*: Volunteer to trade places with one of the children, especially one who has been longing to join the adult table. Enjoy the conversation and smaller chairs. Ask a few leading questions like, "Tell me about that last book you read" or, "What was the worst homework assignment you ever had?" Be a listening adult who really wants to hear what kids say.

One-Minute Treasures

A parent who treasures children understands why Mary "treasured up all these things and pondered them in her heart" (Luke 2:19). A single moment can bring significance and joy, a moment we replay over and over in our minds. Treasuring doesn't always take a lot of time or preparation. A single minute can change an entire day. (HINT: Don't keep the treasuring to yourself; encourage siblings to use ideas like these to treasure each other.)

- *Affirmation Every Day:* Compliment a specific something about each family member every day. Focus on character expression such as: "You thought and prayed through that dilemma well" and "I like the way you talk out your disagreements rather than shout." Occasionally affirm appearance, but let it be aspects the family member can control: "Your smile always lets me know you really care about me" or "You choose clothes that are comfortable yet attractive."
- *Hug and Why*: As you hug your child tell him or her one reason you like to be with him: "I like the way you always have something positive to say about every circumstance."
- *Tell Me About It:* Children love to tell their life events to an audience that doesn't interrupt, interpret, or impose. Listen with rapt attention to how the book report went, what the new friend is like, what made him happy or sad and why. Invite God to guide you to speak on His cue.

- *Roses-Are-Red Poem*: Spontaneously, or over time, compose a poem that tells why you love your child. Set it to the familiar "Roses Are Red," use a limerick form, or make up your own meter. Share it even if it's dismal poetry.
- *Commercial Translation:* At a fun moment recite a commercial that tells why your child is worth more than any amount of money. Perhaps she makes the world more beautiful, brings a clean feeling, or encourages you to do the good you've wanted to do. Pattern your commercial after one familiar to your child.
- *Brag So Your Child Can Hear You:* Some comments go well for all ears: "Mark was so thoughtful that he put away all the dishes without even being asked." Others are best only for your spouse: "Did you know Mark was so calm during his test today that he was able to remember everything he studied?" Let your child know you're proud to talk about him.
- *Beam a Smile and a Nod:* Your child is singing in the church choir or making friends with a new acquaintance, and glances at you for assurance. Reward him with a smile and nod that says, "You're doing great!" and, "Keep up the good work."

Talk It Up

We spend a big portion of every day talking. Whether it's talking to your kids, your spouse, or your friends, make your words count for the good of God.

- *Say It With Detail*: My daughter once left me a note on my computer on a big deadline day. Instead of "Thanks for the note," I said, "Your note made it easier for me to work. All day long I kept reading and rereading it. Thanks." Tell your children exactly why you like what they do, appreciate the attitude they show, treasure the way they are.
- *Hope It Goes Well*: Show interest in your child's activities by asking about them as they depart for the day: "Hope you get a chance to talk with Pat" or "Enjoy your field trip" or "I hope the science test goes well." Let God bless your children through you.
- *How Was It?* Your children will like knowing you not only care before, but after. Hear the happy and the sad, the easy and the

agonizing. Let your child do most of the talking. And encourage your whole family to give each other mutual interest in the details of life.

- *Say It With Celebration*: When things go well say, "All your hard work paid off!" or "I'm so glad that happened."

- *Say It Soothingly but Truthfully*: When things go poorly, assure your child that everybody makes mistakes, that he can find a way to do differently next time, that you're sorry it happened. Saying things that may not be true, such as "It probably wasn't that bad" or "I'm sure yours was the best in the class," devalues your child's experience and your own words.

- *Say It Strictly*: In addition to celebration and reassurance, children also need firm words that give them the boundaries that help your whole family succeed. "I know you don't feel like preparing your project, but last time you felt embarrassed because you didn't put enough time into it. You've got to give it thirty minutes a day, and I have to see results to know you're making the progress you need to make. If you finish in fewer days, you'll have extra afternoons. If things go more slowly, you'll need to spend extra time those last few days."

> The more we practice affirming our children, the faster the word will spread that children really are a treat.

- *Say It Kindly*: Nicely brushed hair and a clean face help children feel good about themselves. But saying, "Get back in that bathroom and scrub again—you look horrible" will definitely defeat your purpose! How about, "Try once more, you missed a spot on your forehead. Look in the mirror before you leave to make sure you get all the dirt."

- *Say the Good You See*: To keep from whining about your children, deliberately speak the good. When someone asks how your children are doing, genuinely say, "Really well—they always come up with some neat way of viewing life that I hadn't thought of." When discussing your teenagers, mention, "It's great to relate to them on a more mature level. We're growing a friendship element to our relationship." When you see other people's children, comment on what you like. "Wow—your Stephanie certainly knows how to make her friends smile." The more we practice affirming our children, the faster the word will spread that children really are a treat.

- *Write Your Words:* Deliver a letter to your child's pillow when he masters his first dentist appointment. Buy a card that tells how much you enjoy being your daughter's daddy. Slip a note to him on the way to tryouts that he can keep in his back pocket.

Fun During Changes

Your three-year-old can now wear big-boy underwear, your preschooler is entering kindergarten, your middle-schooler is shaving her legs for the first time, or your high-schooler is preparing to date. Make these changes more fun and less stressful with a great attitude and by seeing the change from your child's perspective.

- *Be Positive:* Your child is both excited and a little scared about this change. Your attitude will be contagious so choose and display it carefully. "You are a big boy!" is so much better than, "I'm so glad we finally don't have to fool with diapers anymore!" "You have good taste in guys; thanks for choosing caring ones," is so much better than, "I can't believe my baby is dating—I can't handle this!" Any change will likely be hard for you. Admit this, talk with God and your spouse about it, and then move ahead with God's power.
- *Be Private:* When your preschooler is struggling to stop sucking his thumb, don't announce it to the world. Go out to celebrate Woman Day when your young adolescent begins her period— but keep it between you and her, not even telling siblings. When your college-age son fails a significant test, help him discover ways to raise the grade, rather than tell friends at church he's irresponsible. The older your child gets the less comfortable he becomes with your sharing family issues outside the family.
- *Be Funny:* Remembering the laugh-with-not-at rule, lighten up heavy times with a little humor (see Family Funnies box in Chapter 3). "Oh yes, I remember being slammed against the locker five times on my first day of middle school. But I just crawled inside my locker and hid." "But dad! You can't crawl

inside a locker!" This silly interchange brings smiles to the tense preteen who wonders if all the rumors about the much-bigger-than-grade-school are true. Watch your child and know her well enough to know just how much humor to use and just when to use it.

- *Give Fuzzies:* Several years ago the parable of the fuzzies was popular: a fuzzy represented a compliment, an encouragement, a bit of hope to carry along in a tough situation. Hebrews 10:24–25 describes this encouragement-giving process. Sample fuzzies include: "It will be hard this first day but by the end you'll start to feel at home." "I know you'll do a good job on your report because you practiced." "I'll be here praying for you." You might even stick a physical fuzzy in your child's back-pack or lunchbox as a reminder of your love.

- *Give Strategies:* If your child can't remember which books to bring or what assignments are due when, find the method that works for him. Assignment books work great for some, but self-stick notes may work better for your son. Some even prefer writing on their hands. Help him find and use the organization method that works. If your preschooler forgets to pick up her clothes, create a chart or note on the doorknob. Explain: "We all need little reminders to help us do our jobs; let's find what works."

- *That's Thinking Like a Scientist!* Notice and name the good your children do. As she grows interested in science, say, "Your questions show you're thinking like a scientist!" Don't limit such comments to homework time; speak them while in the grocery store, to show that knowledge is everywhere to be found. As he remembers his way around the school, say, "Wow, you're a nav-igating grade-schooler!" As she picks up her clothes consis-tently, say, "You know just how to get things done. What a great picker-upper!"

- *Be a Safety Net:* Together with your teen develop guidelines that help him do the good he wants to do. For example, insist that dating teens only be at the other's house when an adult is in the home. Let your children of all ages blame you when they aren't quite ready to take responsibility for a temptation: "My parents won't let me take more than one passenger in the car."

- *Celebrate:* When your preschooler gets big-boy underwear, go together to the store to buy it and have popcorn in the snack bar. When your fifth-grader completes her first gotta-turn-in-note-cards-too report, go out to play miniature golf together. When your son enters middle school, give him a ring or other piece of jewelry that symbolizes his right and responsibility to make more of his own choices. When your son makes good grades in his first year of high school, make a big banner and cook his favorite foods. On the day your daughter gets her driver's license, give her a set of keys and invite her to drive you to dinner at her favorite restaurant.

- *Put It In Words Together:* Add significance to milestone gifts with a saying you compose together such as, "This ring means I can choose to honor God with people, time, and possessions." Or, "These keys are the key to taking care of people and property with our car." As your child voices the meaning of milestones, she more likely lives that next level of maturity.

- *Prayers for You:* Though listed near the end, this is first in importance, the basis for the 100 other suggestions. Ask God's guidance as you speak every word and take every action with your children. Then tell your children specifically the ways you're praying for them: "I'm praying with you as you build good friends this school year." "I know you have so many things you want to do this summer. I'm praying as you recognize which ones God wants you to do."

Fun That Grows Confidence

One of the most crucial things we do as parents is build our children's confidence as uniquely wonderful creations of God. Some of these actions are ongoing. Others are one-timers that pay off year after year. Most take at least some time and effort, but yield benefits far beyond the hours invested.

- *Secret Kindness:* Draw names without telling which family member you drew. For that week do secret kindnesses for the person whose name you have. You might secretly do a chore, leave notes of affirmation (use your typewriter or computer printer so no one recognizes handwriting), pray for a specific need, tape a favorite TV show and leave it on his bed. If you figure out who's doing your kindnesses, rather than say so, just enjoy. Think of the family harmony that can grow with everyone trying to do more kindness than the other!

- *Have a Portrait Made:* Especially on those years that school pictures don't come out well, schedule a photo-shoot at your local department store. Choose a department store with personnel who enjoy children and treat them with honor. This takes a couple hours and lots of fancying up, but the quality picture that results will please your child or teenager day after day. Use a studio with computer viewing so your child can do instant retakes if a shot doesn't come out. Display the portrait proudly in your home and order enough wallet sizes for your child to exchange freely with friends. This doesn't encourage vanity, but appreciation for a good creation of our good God.

- *Back Off Slowly:* As a second-grader, your child needs your help to digest social studies material for a test. You'll show him the highlighted print that means he needs to remember those words, and the way events fit together. By middle school he can do much of the study on his own, except for quizzing. And by high school he may not even need to show you the book. Grow competence and independence gradually in school work, in decision-making, and in expression of spirituality. Rather than expect a certain pattern, custom-gear this process to each child.

- *Celebrate "You" Day:* My friend Pattie shared this idea with me. A couple months before each senior daughter graduated from high school the family hosted "Celebrate Kristi" night and "Celebrate Kaci" night. They invited all the peers and adults who have contributed to this teen's life to come together and celebrate the first eighteen years. Each guest brings a letter and a blessing. How often do we wait for funerals to gather all the people who mean so much to us, to tell each other why they matter? And then the person can't enjoy it. "Celebrate 'You' Day" shows your child how very many people care about him or her and offers opportunity to thank these people who have helped mold your child into a quality young adult. Once you celebrate one child's life, the others live in anticipation of this life marker. Put the day together to match the personality of your child. As Pattie explains, "Kaci has more friends out of town so I mailed them invitations with an encouragement to make a video message; then we put them all on one tape. It's always harder with those after the eldest because they expect something similar, but you really need to be different. Kaci's party was a month earlier than Kristi's to throw her off-guard. Guests brought a favorite story about the girl and we presented a photo album that showed highlights of her life from birth until the day of the party."

- *Go Watch:* Attend church and school programs, honors ceremonies, ball games, anything your child participates in. Then afterward, always mention at least one thing your child did well.
- *Manage the Mistakes:* Show your child how to move on after a mistake with E.A.S.E. Notice that
  Everybody makes mistakes from time to time. If I could do it
  Again, how would I change it? What do I need to
  Say or do to make this mistake right? And what
  Effort will keep it from happening next time?
  Always assure your child of your love after a mistake, even while you firmly prod him to future excellence.
- *Head Off the Pain:* Use "road signs" to talk about preventing mistakes. Don't just offer warnings; use signs also when you notice your children have prevented pain. "I noticed that you STOPPED rather than spoke ugliness back when he criticized you. You prevented a big fight. Good job!" Other samples: What SLIPPERY conditions will I face and how can I keep from slipping? What does God always give a GO to? What CAUTION will maintain fun while preventing pain? How do I YIELD to good rather than to evil? What CROSSING do I face and which way does God want me to go to stay on the happiness road?
- *How Can I Do Better?* Invite each of your children to name one thing they like about the way you parent and one thing they want you to change. Or invite them to create a report card for you with the subjects of their choice. Insist that they put comments with each grade and suggestions for improvement. Your willingness to hear and learn from them will build trust, earn the right to be heard, and make you a better parent. Of course you'll take some comments with a grain of salt. But the "triple my allowance" comments will be balanced by "just listen to me

when I come to you. I want your guidance but I want to tell you about the problem first."

Joy Tip

Be a miner of ideas. Invite God to guide you to constantly fresh ways to enjoy your children. Then use what you find as guided by God's joyful spirit.

10

WHY DOES IT MATTER, ANYWAY?

Let us hold unswervingly to the hope we profess, for he who promised is faithful. And let us consider how we may spur one another on toward love and good deeds.

—Hebrews 10:23–24

"This enjoying your kids and building up your family stuff sounds great," you might be thinking, "If you have the time and energy to do it. It's fine for full-time moms or dads with nine-to-five jobs. But I don't have that luxury. I work a twelve-hour-a-day job and by the time I get home I don't have the energy for all the things you suggest. It's all we can do to get homework and baths done before bed. We just don't have time for all that extra stuff."

Me either. My husband and I both work ten to twelve hours a day, and we struggle to get the bare basics done most days. On top of that our youngest daughter battles hearing loss and we're constantly having to take unexpected three-hour trips to repair her hearing system or see a doctor. We work daily to overcome hearing hurdles at school, church, and more. Add to that the routine church and school activities of two tireless adolescent girls and we've got one hectic household.

Crazy busyness and overwhelming problems are all the more reason to enjoy your children and grow a family that gets along. Life is too short to miss the things that really matter—growth in Christ and family togetherness. This can seldom be sit-down-in-front-of-the-crackling-fire-and-relax kind of togetherness. Instead it's the while-we're-doing-the-stuff-of-life togetherness.

It's not easy. It's not convenient. But it's crucial.

Why?

Because our children's lives depend on it. Enjoying your kids isn't a choice you make only if you want superkids. It's the choice you make if you want your children to survive. Without a foundation of home-based security, children seek love through status, money, or power. They might join a gang, embrace a boyfriend or girlfriend who presses for sex, or slander their true friends to get into the popular group. Because none of these sources can give what children need—security in Jesus Christ expressed through a family who cares—children without a love foundation experience persistent sadness and restlessness.

With family treasuring and training, our children can have security and joy in any circumstance. They can work as caring members of society rather than join the careening parade of the self-indulgent. They can keep money, power, and status in their places. They can truly enjoy life, people, work, and play. Perhaps most importantly, treasured children become better parents and their God-honoring skills persist through generations to come.

> What we have heard and known, what our fathers have told us. We will not hide them from their children; we will tell the next generation the praiseworthy deeds of the Lord, his power, and the wonders he has done.
>
> He decreed statutes for Jacob and established the law in Israel, which he commanded our forefathers to teach their children, so the next generation would know them, even the children yet to be born, and they in turn would tell their children. Then they would put their trust in God and would not forget his deeds but would keep his commands. They would not be like their forefathers—a stubborn and rebellious generation, whose hearts were not loyal to God, whose spirits were not faithful to him . . . they remembered that God was their Rock, that God Most High was their Redeemer.   Psalm 78:3–8, 35

How can we treasure and enjoy our family in the midst of a crazy schedule? How do we give our children a foundation for a life that matters eternally? While we're running from place to place, we use car time to hear and respond to our kids' experiences of ecstasy and agony. We pray open-eyed prayers for wisdom and courage to do what's right in these circumstances. We provide discipline, strategies, and ideas. We prompt our children to find specific words and actions that honor God in each problem or pleasure. We cultivate caring attitudes that live out joy in the power of Jesus Christ. In all these ways we refuse to make our children the center of attention, but direct them toward the Center of the Universe: God himself.

While our kids do homework, we invest ourselves to make certain they have the study help and school strategies they need to succeed. We show how to write reports or master math problems. We check their homework so they can correct mistakes at home rather than in front of the class. We provide tutors if the material is above our heads. And each time we grow weary with it all, we remind ourselves that as we help up front, we prevent school failures down the line.

While we're grabbing baths and packing lunches for the next day, we purposely take a few moments to anticipate the events our children expect to face the next day. We write reminders to make sure we take the steps that need taking, whether it's buying a ruler for math class, sending money for the field trip, or talking to the friend who's sad. Then we place those reminders where we'll see and heed them—on the car keys for things we do as we go, on the phone for calls to make, on our alarm clock for first-thing-in-the-morning needs.

As we cherish those few quiet minutes to relax at the end of the day, we intentionally notice and speak about how good it is to be tucked in for a cozy night with people who love us. If our children waken in the night, we ponder why they matter rather than whine over why they've dragged us from slumber.

On the way to school and work the next morning we give each child a personal blessing of encouragement: "Do your best on the English test!" "Hope your talk with Terry goes well!" "I'll be praying about that private request." "I'm glad you're a preschooler so we can spend the morning together."

Action by purposeful action, word by caring word, day by crazy day, we equip our children in the business of Christlike living. Life is hard. But we offer the help our kids need to manage it. As we treasure them they notice what's important and work for those real gems in life—companionship, delight, honesty, eternal perspective, all woven together by devotion to God.

Growing a family where people truly like, love, and nurture each other boils down to this: Share life. It starts with how we train *ourselves* to value and enjoy our children, seeing them not as interruptions in our busy parental lives but as fellow humans traveling together with us down the road of life. As our children feel genuinely cared for and discover with us ways to approach all aspects of life with Christlikeness, they grow the faith they need to serve their Savior both now and for eternity:

> Then we your people, the sheep of your pasture, will praise you forever; from generation to generation we will recount your praise.   Psalm 79:13

Joy Tip

Enjoying your kids isn't a choice you make only if you want superkids. It's the choice you make if you want your children to survive physically, emotionally, intellectually, and spiritually.